Aspects of modern sociology

Social processes

GENERAL EDITORS

John Barron Mays
Eleanor Rathbone Professor of Sociology, University of Liverpool

Maurice Craft
Senior Lecturer in Education, University of Exeter

FOR DAVID AND PHILIP

Bureaucracy

Dennis Warwick B.A.

Lecturer in Sociology
University of Leeds

Longman

LONGMAN GROUP LIMITED
London

Associated companies, branches and representatives throughout the world

© *Longman Group Limited 1974*

First published 1974

ISBN 0 582 48008·6 cased
        48009·4 paper

Printed in Hong Kong by
Dai Nippon Printing Co (HK) Ltd

Contents

Editors' Preface

The first series in Longman's *Aspects of Modern Sociology* library was concerned with the social structure of modern Britain, and was intended for students following professional and other courses in universities, polytechnics, colleges of education, and elsewhere in further and higher education, as well as for those members of a wider public wishing to pursue an interest in the nature and structure of British society.

A further series set out to examine the history, aims, techniques and limitations of social research; and this third series is concerned with a number of fundamental social processes. The presentation is each case is basically analytical, but each title will also seek to embody a particular viewpoint. It is hoped that these very relevant introductory texts will also prove to be of interest to a wider, lay readership as well as to students in higher education.

JOHN BARRON MAYS
MAURICE CRAFT

Acknowledgements

We are grateful to the following for permission to reproduce copyright material:
The American Academy of Political and Social Science for an extract from an article by Z Bauman in *Annals* Vol 393, January 1971; The Clarendon Press for an extract from an article by C.R. Hinings in *Sociology* Vol 1 1967, 61–72 and extracts from an article by C.R. Hinings and Gloria L. Lee in *Sociology* Vol 5, 1971, 83–93; Fabian Society for extracts and tables from *Labour and Inequality* edited by Peter Townsend & Nicholas Bosanquet; Her Majesty's Stationery Office for extracts from *Minutes of Evidence No. 5 – Maud Commission on Local Government* and *Minutes of Evidence – Select Committee on Education and Science 1970* and a table based on information from *the Report of the Committee on the Civil Service, Vol 3* and other HMSO publications and table 2 & 3 are compiled from various sources: The Fulton Committee Report, *The Civil Service* Vol 3 (1) HMSO 1969, Tables 3.20, 3.22, 3.33 & 3.35. The Census of England and Wales, General Report, HMSO 1966 and table showing the Social Class of all Economically Active, 1966; Right Honorable Joseph Grimond M.P. for an extract from his article from *Guardian Leader Page*, 21.5.68; General and Municipal Workers' Union for an extract from an advertisement in *Labour Weekly*, 1.9.72; Lawrence & Wishart Ltd for a short quotation from the Foreword of *The UCS Work-in* by W. Thompson and Finlay Hart; National Association of Divisional Executives for Education for an extract from page 54 of *National Association of Divisional Executives for Education Review*, May, 1972; New Statesman for an extract from the front

page of *The New Statesman*, 30.6.72 by General William Westmoreland; The Observer for the article by A. Coote, 'The Shallow End' as appeared in *The Observer Review*, 25.6.72; Pitman Publishing Random House Inc., for specified extracts from *Bureaucracy in Modern Society* by Peter M. Blau and Marshall W. Meyer; Routledge & Kegan Paul Ltd for extract from 'The Two Sociologies' by Alan Dawe as appeared in *British Journal of Sociology*, Vol XXI, No. 2, June 1970; Sociological Review for an extract from an article by A. Giddens in *Sociological Review*, Vol 20 part 3, 1972; The University of Chicago Press for extracts from *The Beaucratic Phenomenon* by M Crozier, 1964 and C.A. Watts & Co Ltd, London for an extract from *Elites and Society* by T.B. Bottomore. Bedminster Press Inc. and M Weber for extracts taken from *Economy and Society* Vols. 1, 2 and 3, 1968.

The author wishes to acknowledge that his intellectual debt is primarily to Alan Dawe. Thanks are also due to Zygmunt Bauman and David Dunkerley for their helpful comments, to the editors of the series for their encouragement, and to Ruth Hemingway who put in many hours of hard work typing the first draft of the book and made many perceptive comments about it.

D.W.

Introduction

SOME POINTS ABOUT DEFINITIONS

Martin Albrow in a recent book called *Bureaucracy* indicates the big problem which exists in attempting to give an overall definition of the concept of bureaucracy. After examining a vast amount of writing in the social and political sciences where the term was used, he concludes that there is 'no element common to them all which could form part of a useful definition'. He goes on:

> When we say that the concepts we have discussed are *related*, we may have found the major information function which the term bureaucracy has. To identify different groups of related human beings we have family names. They are devoid of meaning, but none the less, useful. In the same way, bureaucracy is useful in identifying a range of related problems, i.e. the whole gamut of issues concerning the relations of individuals to abstract organisational features.[1]

Thus he suggests that the term is treated as a kind of signpost concept. It points to an area of social and academic experience which will be seen and defined in different ways according to the different interests involved.

It seems important to start with this point, for it should be made clear that one of the great excitements of the universe of discourse, which we call sociology, is that there is little agreement about the meanings of the concepts or terms that we use to form the reference points around which an explanation of social action can be given. The basic reason for this is, as Coulson and Riddell point out, that 'there are ... very big disagreements among sociologists about orientations to the subject, and about the attitude that should be taken to the disagreements themselves'.[2] In addition, as Alan Dawe has argued, sociologists may change their orientations to their subject during their working life so that there may not be consistency about the use and meaning of particular concepts within the works of such a sociologist.[3]

In some ways, too, the decision of the editors of this series to invite a contribution on bureaucracy within a set of works on social processes may be looked on as conceptually confusing. The notion which the term 'social process' attempts to capture is the sense of the dynamic in social life, sequences of action, often repeated and possibly patterned, by which individuals and groups seek to achieve particular goals. Social processes as dynamic aspects of social life tend also to be set against 'social structures' or notions about the relatively static way in which relationships between individuals and groups are patterned and ordered and come to be part of the consciousness of people. Bureaucracy has been used in so many ways that it is impossible to put it into either the category of structure or that of process. Indeed, if we look at Albrow's discussion of the concept, it is clear that interpretations of bureaucracy may fall within one of these categories, across them or even outside them. Albrow suggests that there are seven modern concepts of bureaucracy:[4]

1. *Bureaucracy as rational organisation*
When it is used in this way, the writer is usually concerned with the analysis of the methods used by sets of people who are appointed or who have come together voluntarily to pursue in organised fashion a common purpose or purposes. Some assumptions are usually made about what constitutes rational organisation and the analysis tends to be in terms of the extent to which the observed methods are rational in consequence. This approach tends to be defined as managerial for fairly obvious reasons. Such 'use of the concept of bureaucracy would suggest its categorisation as a social process.

2. *Bureaucracy as organisation inefficiency*

This use of the concept tends to be a variant of the first form. Again writers are concerned more with the process of administration than with a structure, but here make the assumption that the needs of modern industrial and commercial enterprises are not well served by a bureaucratic system. Albrow gives Michel Crozier and his book *The Bureaucratic Phenomenon* (1964) as an example (see below, chapter 4).

3. *Bureaucracy as rule by officials*

Albrow indicates that this definition coincides with the earliest use of the concept, where the predominant question of the writers was concerned with the distribution of power in society. In this sense, bureaucracy comes to be seen as an elite group, having considerable control over the lives and fortunes of the other members of a society. This use of the concept puts it outside the notions of both structure and process, although it can obviously be seen as an element of structure.

4. *Bureaucracy as public administration*

This use of the concept is said by Albrow to derive from a work by Michels[5] which caused later writers to see bureaucracy as a part of any organisation structure. Here the bureaucracy is defined, not as the elite group, but as an influential group, or a pressure group, related by their common interest as employees of the state, local authorities, or public corporations. This fourth concept of bureaucracy can be categorised in the same way as the third.

5. *Bureaucracy as administration by officials*

Max Weber, it is argued by Albrow, never made explicit the full range of concepts which he used when discussing bureaucracy.[6] Albrow contends that he had a general concept which amounts to administration by appointed officials, and suggests that supporting evidence for this idea comes from other writers who have closely followed the Weberian analysis. The use of the concept in this way focuses attention both on the process by which an organisation

3

is run and on the structure of relationships within it. Further, bureaucracy has been the starting point for analysis of change in the form of organisations so that for example a change in the ratio of non-manual to manual workers, has been taken as an index of bureaucratisation.

6. *Bureaucracy as the organisation*
It can be seen that the use of the concept in the fifth form makes easy a shift to considering the whole organisation as a bureaucracy. The more an organisation becomes bureaucratised, the more nearly is the whole structure affected by the administrational hierarchy. Many modern writers thus refer to modern organisations like schools, colleges, churches, and hospitals and even sports clubs, as well as large-scale industrial and commercial concerns, as bureaucracies. In this sense it is a structural concept.

7. *Bureaucracy as modern society*
Further elaboration of the concept of bureaucratisation and concern with the growth of scale in modern organisations has led many writers to characterise modern industrial societies as bureaucracies. In this case too, bureaucracy is a structural concept, and bureaucratisation becomes an aspect of social processes.

Just to reinforce this point about the difficulty of maintaining conceptual clarity and labelling bureaucracy as structure or process, let us look at the following extract from *Bureaucracy in Modern Society* by Peter Blau and Marshall Meyer:

> The type of organisation designed to accomplish large-scale administrative tasks by systematically co-ordinating the work of many individuals is called a bureaucracy. This concept, then, applies to organising principles that are intended to improve administrative efficiency and that generally do so, although bureaucratisation quite often has the opposite effect of producing inefficiency. Since complex administrative problems confront most large organisations, bureaucracy is not confined to the military and civilian branches of the government, but is also found in business, unions, churches, universities, and even in baseball clubs.

Interestingly enough, while the term bureaucratic is often used as a synonym for inefficiency, at other times, it is used to imply ruthless efficiency. Some of the radical criticism of contemporary society, particularly by the New Left, tends to blame bureaucratic institutions for all the evils in today's world. . . . There is an element of truth in this criticism, for the bureaucratic form of organisation is an effective instrument that helps powerful groups to dominate others, thereby engendering alienation and endangering democracy. However, the criticism is misleading. . . . Karl Marx himself, though he condemns bureaucracy in several passages, clearly considers the power differences in the class structure, not bureaucracy, responsible for oppression, exploitation, and alienation.

Bureaucracies are powerful institutions which greatly enhance potential capacities for good or for evil, because they are neutral instruments of rational administration on a large scale.[7]

In this extract, Blau and Meyer seem to shift from one concept to another, if we accept Albrow's classification. In the first sentence, they seem to prefer a concept close to type five, *Bureaucracy as administration by officials*, but a claim could be made that since they use the indefinite article before bureaucracy in the first sentence, they are moving to type 6, *Bureaucracy as the organisation*. Certainly, they seem to end with the type 6 concept, but in their reference to unions, churches and clubs, they talk of bureaucracy *in* them, which ties up with the reference to organising principles and efficiency as type 1, *Bureaucracy as rational organisation*. They do not dismiss type 2, *Bureaucracy as organisational inefficiency*, entirely, and in the reference to New Left criticism there is more than a hint of type 3, *Bureaucracy as rule by officials*.

There are two things to be said, arising from this. *One* is that Blau and Meyer are concerned to capture within their discussion of bureaucracy as much information as they can. They recognise that bureaucracy is a socially produced phenomenon, and that individuals and groups in varying positions in a society will define it differently. The purpose of their book seems, however, to be somewhat ambiguous. On the one hand they seem to want

5

to preserve social institutions and order, by making the bureaucracy work better, but on the other hand, they share a concern with the New Left that bureaucracies might be oppressive. 'If we want to utilise efficient bureaucracies, we must find democratic methods of controlling them lest they enslave us'.[8] This possibly explains why they find it impossible to preserve conceptual clarity, measured in Albrow's terms. The *second* is that it seems probable that no sociologist will ever maintain throughout an analysis a consistency with regard to any of Albrow's types of bureaucracy, if he is concerned for instance to include within the account some reference to the varying definitions of the situation, held by participants. In other words, there is really no point in talking about conceptual clarity, except in relation to the enterprise in which the sociologist is concerned.

This brings us right back to the point that I made in the beginning. It all depends on the interests which are involved. Thus it is incumbent on the author to say something about his own aims and interests.

THE SOCIOLOGICAL CONTEXT OF THE BOOK

Every sociologist is born in a social group and experiences involvement probably in many others. His own consciousness of this social experience will enter into every future work situation and will lead him, despite willingness to introduce checks, in the form of reference to other experiential accounts, to make choices about subject matter and the way to look at it. He can never stand outside his experience and dispassionately assess it. As also the subject matter of the sociologist is human life and the effect of social experience on the way that humans act, which is the concern of every other person and the source of problems about which many have felt deeply to the extent of being willing to enter open conflict, 'the sociologist cannot avoid the problem of social values in his work.'[9]

The basic value position in which this work starts is that we must see man as a choice-making and intentional actor—not just a role-player acting in relation to externally held expectations and entirely determined by system imperatives over which he has no control. This is not to deny the existence of role-playing in everyday life nor the coordination of life activities, sometimes in an imperative manner, by forces which seem outside our control. Indeed, we must take into account the continuous process in which individuals and groups interact and attempt to constrain each other to act in socially approved ways. The sociologist cannot, however, overlook the tensions in social life arising from the clash of projected purposive action and social constraint. Hence, the work is also based on the following assumptions:

1. Man's acts derive from goals which relate to his social consciousness or the meaning he attaches to his general social situation.
2. This social consciousness is derived from his interaction with other men and depends on social learning and instruction in its widest sense, or socialisation.
3. Socialisation depends on the range of experiences which are possible for each individual and the groups to which he belongs.
4. Socialisation is a complex process in which the individual plays an active part, and continues throughout life.
5. The range of experiences in which socialisation takes place is limited for individuals and groups of which they are members by the pattern of relationships between groups and the way that these change, that is, by the social structure of a particular society.
6. Where some groups attain dominance over others, within a social structure, their established ways of doing things, the ideas, claimed values and principles of selection in which these established ways are based and the means in language and forms of language by which they are communicated—that is, their culture—tend to emerge as the dominant culture. Social structure and culture have a complex interrelationship with each other.

In stating these starting points for analysis, the author is following fairly closely the position taken by Coulson and Riddell in their book *Approaching Sociology*. The emphasis is to be placed on action and interaction in a dynamic analysis and 'if we are concerned with the interrelations over time of groups of people in social structures, then we *are* trying to understand *processes from interactions in structures*'.[10] Thus when looking at the phenomenon of bureaucracy we shall not be concerned with the problem of whether it is structure or process, but how it is related to the way in which social processes can be explained.

This kind of approach does not let us fall into the trap of assuming, on the one hand, that there are inevitable consequences for man in bureaucracy, or, on the other hand, that it is a thing in itself which lies outside man's control. Studies have often made these two kinds of mistake of being too deterministic or, secondly, of reifying a central concept. It will be the aim here to ask how far bureaucracies and bureaucratisation are no more than means used by dominant groups to maintain their own position of dominance. Also, is it the case that individuals and groups appointed to work in bureaucracies will tend to use them to further their own ends, such as access to elite membership or status mobility?

The approach to the answers to these questions will involve looking at the extent to which the experience, the practical theorising, the interests and the commitments of a person come into the images of the world that he produces. Various images of bureaucracy will be considered, starting with one which is very central to the author. Then we will approach the difficult task of trying to present a reasonably short account of the way that sociologists in general have approached the study of images of bureaucracy. Here we shall start with Max Weber, since most of the recent studies revolve principally around him and to some extent arise as a kind of debate with Weber. In the last two chapters, we shall consider some of the implications of this account and the attempt to formulate an appropriate framework for sociological analysis, in looking at education and modern Britain.

Images of bureaucracy

The collection of material really starts when a problem begins to confront the sociologist. In the case of understanding or attempting to act in relation to what people call bureaucracy, the problem which really started the author considering and, therefore, collecting evidence about it, was one which was a public issue of the 1960s. It was the question of control and participation in a college in the higher education sector. Awareness of the problem grew partly from reading and teaching sociology, and partly from taking part in constructing a form of staff government for the college at the same time as a staff/student committee in the sociology department. On the one hand there was the knowledge of social structure, of competing groups and ideologies and of tactics and strategies by which some groups legitimated their dominance and inequalities of access to power and control and others deferred to or challenged them. On the other hand there was participation in a similar kind of process in a microstructure, where the conflicting pressures of real individuals and groups impinged on the consciousness in different and time-consuming ways.

The staff and students who formed this microstructure (a college of education for student teachers) at the end of the 1960s numbered about 900, a fifth of whom were staff (tutorial, administrative, clerical, technical, catering and so on). The students were predominantly women; fewer than one in five were men. A large proportion of the students had entered college at the age of eighteen; about one in five entered at the age of twenty-five or older. Of this latter set, most were married and resident in the urban zone around the college. About half of the younger students were resident in the college campus. Thus in terms of very obvious categories the student groups were differently structured from those in other kinds of higher education institutions, but very similar to those in other urban colleges of education. University and polytechnic student groups have a predominance of males and on the whole are more highly qualified, in terms of examination results, than college students. In terms of the wider social structure, the college was felt to have a low status with reference to other parts of higher education, because of its female and somewhat maternal image and its lower entry requirements.

Like other colleges, its status was closely tied to that of school teachers, particularly those teaching children in lower age ranges and of lesser ability. Such teachers through their unions had constantly sought to raise their collective status to lift themselves above the servile image which they considered they had in the nineteenth century and in the first half of the twentieth. One of the strategies involved in this drive for higher status was the extension of the teacher training course from two to three years, to give it more prestige and comparability with other courses in higher education. The success of this strategy coincided with the recognition by educational administrators of a short supply of teachers, especially women, to meet contemporary staffing standards in schools in the early 1960s. The effect of this on the college, like all other colleges, was experienced in the increasing numbers of staff and students, an increase from about 300 members in 1960 to 900 in 1969.

The teaching staff of the college recruited in the 1960s tended to be men rather than women, whereas previously the staff were mainly women, like the students. This was a consequence of the recognition of the college of education as an alternative for career advance for men teachers as well as a cultural change resulting from structural pressures, which enabled members of appointing committees to change their norms about the suitability of men teachers for women students, at the same time as receiving many more applications for jobs from men than women. The trend in the appointments at this time, too, was towards the creation of groups of teachers of arts and sciences, rather than of education and methods of practical teaching. This was a consequence of the interpretation of the notion of giving more prestige to the training course. It was a move in the direction of high status knowledge (i.e. stressing academic rather than vocational aspects of the course), but it also created the opportunity for teaching staff to coalesce as departments around particular subject labels.

The drive for higher status, the increase in the number of members of the college, the increasing 'maleness' of the teaching staff and the development of teaching departments were all aspects of the complex change affecting the consciousness of staff and students, which in turn produced more change. Clearly, the college was implicated in a process which had both external and internal dimensions. Perhaps the most crucial of these have still to be mentioned.

For the teachers in the college, and in many other colleges, the experiences of rising status in some aspects was dissonant with other experiences. Ultimate control of the college lay outside the college. Local authorities controlled day-to-day expenditure, the central government through its Department of Education officials and advisers controlled long-term development and the university controlled academic standards and the certification of students. Local authority members and officials, often being in closest proximity to the college compared with members of the other organisations, perhaps were symbolic of the cause of this dissonance. Teachers in colleges certainly pressed for the end of local authority control, and their arguments were embodied in an official report on higher education in 1963.[1] The recommendations of the members of the Higher Education Committee, for the incorporation of colleges into the university structure and for the reorganisation of higher education into a unified system, centrally controlled, were based on much wider issues than that of the status of colleges. They involved, however, structural and cultural changes for the colleges which the supporters of the recommendations at that time had no power to produce, such as the reduction of the sphere of competence of local education authorities and the greater involvement of universities in the professional education of members of an occupation that still had a very marginal status (in that there were conflicting arguments about it). In other words, the power lay with groups that legitimated their dominance with reference to traditional arguments—the autonomy of local government and the primacy of theoretical enterprise in the university—as well as to more pragmatic ones about the costs of such administrative changes. Much negotiation followed, and in this concessions were made by local authorities, so that legislation made possible, at least theoretically, the achievement of some symbols of autonomy and improving status in the colleges to match those of the longer courses, and the B.Ed. degree which some students were allowed to take after 1965. Specifically, these were the appointment of a senior administrative officer on the college staff and the setting up of a form of academic government by the teaching staff. The local authorities still retained financial control, reinforced by agreements about pooling resources between authorities, and policy control through retaining power of appointment of a majority of the members of the governing body of the college.[2] In the college with which this account is concerned the events of the arrival of a senior administrative officer and the formation in 1967 of an academic board, largely consisting of members who held senior positions on the teaching staff, brought awareness of a considerable emphasis on formality and hierarchy in decision-making, and reinforced the tendency to make discussion and documentation about policy and procedures also matters for considerable debate and regulation.

This development was again not entirely the product of external forces acting on the college. Within the college, in the period of change, several older members of the teaching staff in senior positions retired, and were replaced, in some cases at least, by new members from outside. These, by bringing different orientations to the college, often exercised influence in shifting attitudes of the rest towards acceptance of the new departmental developments, which have been mentioned above, and in appointing other new members of staff with more readiness to accept the more formal conditions, or with more willingness to recognise that alternative forms of control and procedure could be envisaged. Thus there was a considerable increase in discussion and negotiation about the purpose of the college, in terms of the education and training of teachers, the means by which such educational purposes should be achieved, the expectations that should be held for different departments and groups of teachers within the college, and the means by which the college should be organised administratively to deal with the process. Varying definitions of the situation emerged which individuals and groups attempted to impose on the rest. The academic board and the academic council—the latter a meeting of all college teachers which officially only had an advisory role and was subordinate to the academic board—became the institutionalised means for the process of negotiation and for the resolution of conflicts. The facts that the academic board and council were linked by legislation to the formal structure of control of the college through the local authority, and, through the Department of Education and Science at central government level, to the state, and that the same legal structure confirmed and sanctioned the appointment of college teachers and imposed a hierarchical structure on them, which was reinforced by salary differentials, meant that negotiations were always conditioned by these legal sanctions.

The way the negotiations were conditioned did, however, depend on the interpretation of the legal structure made by the most senior members of the academic hierarchy. This could vary, for on some occasions it was defined as manipulable, and on others it was defined as rigid and inflexible. The choice of such definitions depended to some extent on the power of the senior members to control the information which more junior members had of the legal structure, and on whether it suited the interests of the senior members to use the more flexible or the more rigid definition. For instance, they would use the more flexible model when some proposed change in the college seemed to them desirable—for example, a small innovation such as a seminar on the education of immigrant children, which might gain some recognition for the college in the teaching world. On the other hand, they would use the more rigid concept of the legal structure when some proposal for a change did not seem desirable to them—such as a request for students to be represented in more than a token sense in the academic government of the college. When a rigid definition was being used as a sanction within a set of negotiations, the individuals and groups involved in making the unacceptable proposals were then made clearly conscious of the reverberations that might occur throughout the structure should such proposals be pressed. The sanction of the legal structure clearly could then be very effective in restraining some proposed changes, because without the support of senior members the possibility of gaining support from powerful members of the legal structure—for example, in the local authority or the central government—was very unlikely. In addition, junior members and even marginal or unorthodox senior members depended on the legal structure for their style of life and its future possibilities in the form of regular salary and career prospects, so that a continued challenge to the local embodiment of that legal structure would rarely seem worth while. In the college, as time went on, it thus became increasingly obvious that the changes in the official structure giving it something of the status of an autonomous organisation restricted the experience of that autonomy to a few of the members only. The outcome was somewhat centralised decision-making and an arbitrariness about the process in the view of those not continually part of the dominant coalition[3] of senior members.

This awareness of the tendencies towards formality, the growth of hierarchies and departmentalism, codification of rules, increased use of written communications, rigidity in the face of radical innovation, centralisation of decision-making and a growing sense of remoteness, which arbitrariness tends to create, is comparable to the experience of many others who have used the concept of bureaucracy to sum up and generalise their analysis. In the case of the author, the experience was mediated through an awareness of such sociological analysis and it therefore became a problem as to how far such analysis was meaningful. How far did it represent a reality to which other members of the college were also responding?

THE IMAGE VALIDATED?

In the first place, of course, the experience was based on interaction with other members of the college, and with members of other colleges and organisations which in various ways were involved in the work of the author, such as official boards of studies at the local university and meetings and committees of the Association of Teachers in Colleges and Departments of Education. It was from this interaction that the notion of the essential human origin of the process derived, of the existence of goals and the use of energy in the attempt to achieve such goals. It also formed a basis for a subjective comparative analysis of experiences, which tended to confirm not only the various aspects of the bureaucratisation of the college, but also the interpretation of the internal and external forces at work on the process. Another outcome of the interaction was a recognition of the variability of the process in different colleges, which were part of the same legal structure, which tended to add weight to the point made above about the importance of the interpretations of the legal structure made by the senior members of the college hierarchies. It also suggested that another source of the variation might be in the way that such senior members were subject to variable interpretations of the legal structure passed down to them from the various and somewhat conflicting external groups involved in the control of the college.

Secondly, some judgment of the validity of the author's analysis can be derived from records of events and interaction, and from documents and pamphlets which convey a written reminder of the views of members of the college. Among the events that were closely related to the process, the arrival of the senior administrative officer has already been mentioned. In the year following his arrival, a complete reorganisation of the administration involved the specification in offical pronouncements of the ways in which staff and students should and should not be involved in contact with members of the clerical and administrative staff. The growth in the size of the membership of the college entailed a larger number of files to be kept, and there was a complete re-equipping of the offices with new filing systems. But it was the way that these events were interpreted by other members of the college, rather than the very fact of them, that led to the validation of the notion of bureaucratisation. The specifications tended to be issued as edicts from on high, rather than as the product of discussions that were made public. As a result, the new 'regulations' confronted the former norms about contacting the clerical and administrative staff. The confrontation emphasised the attempt to create a gap in the membership of the college, and to isolate one set of activities and members from others. This particular gap was emphasised even more by the decision of the members of the academic board not to allow the senior administrative officer to attend their meetings, even though his knowledge and control of a part of the activities of the college would often have brought to such meetings information that could have been useful, or at least could have been defined as useful.

Other gaps, too, came to be more obvious as the negotiations which have been noted above highlighted areas of disagreement between individuals and groups in the college. The negotiations, apart from being institutionalised in the various boards and committees which were set up, tended to become almost ritualised, in that the same point of disagreement would come up over and over again, and the same kind of discussion would follow, so that the means of solving disputes, meetings in committee or in departments, became the ends: meetings for the sake of meetings. That this was a common definition of the situation can be judged from the usual laughter that followed statements such as 'going to another meeting' or 'meetings are becoming a habit at this college' when used as opening gambits in a conversation. The very ritual of meetings, however, affected the consciousness of members to the extent that there seemed to be no way of changing things, of closing gaps for instance, and all that remained was for different interest groups to take up a posture of being for a gap or against it. One such gap, and a focus of discussion at innumerable meetings, was that between college teachers and students, and the issue which structured it most of all was that of assessment. On the one hand, there were repeated appeals for 'more community spirit' from both teachers and students. Thus a document, published by ATCDE and adopted by the college teachers for discussion, stated:

> There should be staff-student consultation on all major matters that affect the work and welfare of students and of the college community as a whole. We would expect to find in every college open, informal and friendly consultation at all levels between students and tutors as individuals and we think that there ought also to be formal consultation and participation within the college.[4]

The college magazine, in an editorial commented, 'The main thing is for lecturers and students to get used to being in close proximity to one another. Possibly if they used the same lavatories it would help, since there is something in the English nature that makes people talk there.'[5] On the other hand, there was acceptance that there were some things that could not be discussed communally. The same ATCDE document, while recommending that formal consultation meant that students should be on committees with teachers, pointed out that it was inappropriate for students to be present at committee meetings when there was 'discussion of the progress, well-being and assessment of individual students'.

Students, at the same time as accepting assessment as a necessary feature of their education, seemed on the whole to want to use the fact of its necessity as means of bargaining for some improvement in their position. An exchange of views on this topic is recorded in the account of a departmental meeting held in the same year:

Students:
Work handed in for assessment by tutors is frequently retained for a length of time considered unreasonable by many students. . . . There is a strong feeling that essays are not read in depth by tutors

and, consequently, assessments are not reliable guides to the quality of the work or the progress of the student. Tutors should accept a time limit for assessing and returning essays, which should not exceed half a term. The head of the department should do a percentage random check of work handed in for assessment. Some insight concerning how assessment is made should be given either to the groups concerned or to their group representatives for passing on.
Staff (reply as reported by students):
The comments concerning the length of time that work is retained by tutors for assessment were noted and a time limit was accepted in principle. It was thought, and deplored, that there might be an element of truth in the suggestion that essays were not read in depth by individual lecturers, but if this occurred it was due to pressure. In any case, the department felt that there tended to be too much concern given by students to assessment. The department was . . . not too concerned that assessment should always be at a high level. . . . Next year, it was intended to introduce cross marking in order that the staff have some common measure against which to assess each group's essays.

The students, while accepting the principle of assessment, clearly were more interested in making it more difficult for staff to assess their work badly, by pointing to the considerable deficiencies in the means adopted. What might seem to be the crucial point, however, on the insight into the methods used, was not answered by the staff, and the point was not apparently pressed. Other points were conceded, but by stressing the over-concern of students in assessment, presumably the staff were attempting to suggest that it was the students now who were rocking the community boat, and that it would be better if things stayed as they were.

Such discussions were possibly repeated in several departments, but apart from momentary losses of temper, such as when one student ventured to suggest that in some cases assessment occurred so mysteriously that it might seem that 'a black hand gang' could be at work, the legal structure tended to assert itself and the notion of the gap between staff and students entered more deeply into the consciousness of the members of the college. It would seem indeed that the appeals to the idea of community were accepted as reminders of the legal structure, but at the same time as sweeteners which took attention away from the somewhat stern reality of the structure in which the college was integrated. This would only be revealed if the members of the college, or some groups of them, attempted to pursue the task of asking basic questions and demanding changes in the way in which assessment and the wider, but related, issues of participation and control, were regulated. This was the case in several colleges and universities, between 1968 and 1970,[6] but on the whole the majority of members of the college here being considered seemed to accept the structure of the college as it was, with its gaps, its arbitrariness, its hierarchies, its departments, and so on. The college was at least something which offered some prospects of career advance for college teachers, and in every case it offered them security of tenure if they did not challenge it too far. For the students, it did provide reasonable certainty of qualified teacher status in the end, even if they could not be certain how this happened.

These seem to be crucial points to be underlined, that even if members of an organisation, like the college, do see the process of interaction leading to bureaucratisation, but feel satisfied that they can achieve the goals that seem important to them, such as career advance, reasonable security, or a desired qualification, then the definition of bureaucracy is not necessarily one which will excite much response. It is when the issue of control or loss of it becomes a part of the consciousness of individuals and groups in an organisation, and when the maintenance, retention or achievement of control is a real goal, that concern arises about the way in which decisions are being taken, about the distribution of influence, about the way in which stability is preserved and about the way in which change is engendered. Questions about bureaucracy are ultimately questions about power.

THE IMPLICATIONS OF THE IMAGE OF A COLLEGE

The description and analysis of the college has given us a glimpse of what bureaucracy might mean. Let us summarise some of the evidence:

1. Bureaucracy is a concept which is used to capture the notion of a social structure which confronts most members of an organisation and possibly prevents them from feeling able to be any more than subordinates without any real control over the social processes which are going on in the organisation.
2. Bureaucracy is also a concept which evokes the process whereby members have their position and degree of subordinacy defined, their jobs categorised, separated and changed, and the manner in which they relate to other members of the organisation regulated.
3. Bureaucracy is a concept, in addition, which points directly at the nexus of control in an organisation, the members who make the decisions and are responsible for initiating activity, and the source of moves to retain centralised power and rigid rules.
4. The bureaucracy in this third sense is fundamentally supported and sanctioned by a legal structure (with its apparatus of law enforcement) which is an element of the wider society in which organisation is placed. The bureaucracy as such may, however, to some extent be able to control the definition of this legal structure held by the subordinates, and use it as a means of negotiating with them about changes in the process (defined in 2 above).
5. This process may seem to be controlled by the central decision-makers but its degree of pervasiveness may be defined in various ways by the members of the organisation, in accordance with the goals which they bring to the situation and their perceived success in achieving them. Feelings of frustration, remoteness and arbitrariness, often attributed to bureaucracy, will arise in relation to members' own perception of success or failure with regard to their goals.

In the next chapter, we must look at the way that bureaucracy has been treated by sociologists, but before that, it will be useful to look at some other images of bureaucracy.

OTHER IMAGES

The first two of these other images are drawn from analyses made in relation to the period of student activism in the late 1960s.

I

I don't know why students revolt. But I know of several good reasons why they should. They should revolt against bureaucracy in all its forms and attitudes, against bureaucracy in government, in big business, in the parties' apparatus among students themselves, in the professions. They should revolt against the mind which thinks only in terms of the organisation to which it belongs or the fashions with which it has been indoctrinated. Against technical and economic determinism. Against the use of education to turn out slaves for a machine-driven technocracy. Against professors who spend a minimum time in the Universities where they are supposed to teach. Against the doings of the public relations world in which politics are reduced to a confidence trick or a branch of psephology in which the individual is drained of individuality by dependence on subsidies, prestige and the quest for perks and consumer goods. Against the world of government where "experts" proliferate and inefficiency abounds; the world where people find their lives shattered not by earthquake or revolution, but by some bolt from the Government decided upon in secret, the brain-child of some clever theoretician or bureaucratic lobby, irreversible and disastrous. . . .

Not all students accept that British bureaucracy is the answer to the world's trouble. They believe that they could do better. They want to take a more continuous part in discussing our aims and in the direction of government, the professions and business. They want a more equal and a more democratic society. At least I hope they do. I hope they stand for democracy against bureaucracy: for man against machine; for open against secret decision-making; for humanity against prestige; in the phrase from the title of a recent book—for life against death.[7]

II

The point is that the social world appears to us every day like a giant leaden globe turning with a crushing and inevitable weight nothing can alter; our ideas and enthusiasms, our visions, appear like flimsy muslin by contrast, a smoke of feelings with no purchase on fact. Then, in the revolutionary situation, it is seen and felt that this is utterly, radically untrue. Alienation *is* this very idea: the feeling of being a passenger in a lead world one has no power over. The irresistible leaden force *is* only our absence from the turning mass. And we are absent, because we can't think of being present. Then when an act of presence—a revolution—is accomplished, among any considerable number of people, they realise the comic truth. All they have to do is breathe heavily in approximate unison and the thing stops. Touch it, and it disintegrates like Humpty-Dumpty beyond possibility of repair, carrying all the snorting, pipe-puffing realism of the world with it in a pile of rubble.[8]

The first of these by a former leader of the British Liberal Party takes what might be called an orthodox antibureaucratic position. It is difficult to know whether this arises out of his experiences of seeking for several years unsuccessfully to gain electoral support for his party, but clearly this must have provided him with many feelings of frustration and lack of control, which could have been generalised into a theory seeking to explain the situation without having to specify individuals and groups. Bureaucracy in this sense provides the label around which a whole gamut of perceived evils can be defined, blame allocated and the soul of man resurrected. The statement is at once both a catharsis, an act of freeing the mind by an emotional outburst, and a battle cry, hoping to arouse the troops to the banner once more. Of course, bureaucracy was very much at this time part of the demonology of the student left, and as the British Government was engaged in giving the vote (by reducing the voting age from twenty-one to eighteen) to students, there was some point in appealing to them in this way. Apart from this, however, the piece does contain all the elements of the anti-bureaucratic theory:

1. bureaucracy has infiltrated the whole world;
2. bureaucracy emphasises dehumanisation, for it raises the machine above man;
3. bureaucracy then gives man false goals, by encouraging the pursuit of prestige, rather than humanity;

4. bureaucracy cuts off people from making the decisions which affect their lives; and, therefore,
5. bureaucracy must be replaced by democracy, which by implication does not do these things to man.

The second piece, in the form that it was published, as part of one of the documents of the Hornsey College of Art 'revolution' in 1968, was significantly interleaved with two black-and-white reproductions of posters of the 'revolution', announcing:

BUREAUCRACY—SMASH THE SYSTEM
BUREAUCRACY MAKES PARASITES OF US ALL.

The posters and the piece together emphasise what seem to be contradictions in both the manifestations and the theory of bureaucracy. When we have cause to present ourselves to an organisation as outsiders, seeking a service, making a claim, wanting a job, or being compelled to do something, the organisation can seem to be massive, impenetrable and unstoppable. At other times, we can feel that it is just the opposite, 'like a ball of cotton wool', as a member of a school parents' committee said of the local education authority when he was trying to press home a case about that authority's inability to control the contractors in building a new school. In other words, the members of a bureaucracy seem to be able to present different definitions of the situation to an outsider according to the way that the outsider is defined by them. Theoretically, bureaucracy can be defined as something real and external to man, which can significantly impose its definitions on him and constrain his actions; but it can also be defined as just an image held by man, an image which is shared, but which can be destroyed by a conscious act of will on the part of the purposive groups. The 'system' is symbolic of this external constraining reality, which 'makes parasites of us all' but which 'nothing can alter'. By thinking radically, however, and by forgetting to act parasytically, we can overcome our alienation, our separation from our true humanity. But in so far as theoretically it is at one moment something external and at another something entirely internal, there is a contradiction in the argument, which must be resolved. It is not so easy to make bureaucrats resolve the contradictory image they present to us, but at least we can attribute this to their irrationality, and in future not expect them to be rational. With theoreticians it is perhaps different. We have some right to expect that some consistency be maintained. Our theoreticians of the Hornsey 'revolution' might have added that, even if the 'giant leaden globe' was an image, the sets of people, individuals and groups, were real members of the system, involved in social relationships which had some stability and structure about them. Thinking would not remove them. It is by social action that we can confront and change a social system.

Student revolutions have not of course been the only events to have evoked thoughts about bureaucracy, but clearly the issues of 1968 have not been forgotten by one student activist of the time. Miss Anna Coote, the editor of the Edinburgh University student newspaper in 1968, and prominent according to *The Observer* in the activism of that institution at that time,[9] recently contributed to the same newspaper an article which has obvious links with the analysis of earlier days.

III

Work begins at 9.15 a.m. If you are late you get reported to the office manager. There is a bunch of files and a full tape waiting in the basket by the desk. You switch on the machine, slot in the cassette, plug in the ear-phones, insert paper-carbon-paper, place foot on pedal and off you go. It is a small pool. My desk is arranged so that I face a large pillar with my back to the rest of the girls. The voices tunnelling into my head belong to two women who work in the accounts department. Occasionally I see them walking past my desk. They nod and smile to me twice a day when they put new work in the basket. The letters and memos are usually half a page long and their message founders in abominable jargon: 'Dear sir, we would refer to your letter of the 13th instant and regret the delay in replying thereto. . . . ' I produce about 30 variations of this each day—one copy to be hoarded as proof that something has been done, another to swell the work load of the GPO and the filing systems of other offices just like mine. If you make a mistake you can cover it with

Tipp-ex and nobody notices. If you make a big mistake you can type the letter again and nobody notices. If you make no mistakes the result is the same. If you do six tapes a day instead of the average three, you sit there with nothing to do, which is worse after a while. There is no earthly way of excelling.

The office hierarchy screams at you. The typing pool is on the lowest floor with the junior executives, trainees and male clerks. The men sit at one end of the open plan office next to the large windows. The typists sit at the dingy end with the filing cabinets. The copy typist who sits with the men and gets their coffee for them enjoys more prestige than the girls in the pool. The senior executives sit upstairs. So do their secretaries, who seldom exchange words with the typists. The typists are told not to talk loudly or giggle when they fetch their coffee from the upstairs office. It is rumoured that directors work on the floor above.

At lunch-time we eat crispbread and cheese spread at our desks (1 15p luncheon voucher won't stretch much further) while the men troop off to the local restaurant. There is a minor feud in the pool. The homely girls who talk endlessly of engagements, weddings, HP and in-laws, resent the dolly birds who get chatted up by the men they type for. None of the girls wants to stop work when they get married. But they look upon marriage as something to give their lives purpose and divert attention from the work they do for eight hours each day. I asked what prospects the job held for me. The office manager looked surprised. 'You never know,' he said, 'one day there could be a vacancy for a secretary to one of our directors.' He might have been offering me the moon.[10]

This is presumably how it is! It is interesting to note that one of the letters received and published by *The Observer* following this article did encourage secretaries to join a union, but other comments mainly attacked the supposition that secretaries could not work their way up the hierarchy. This attack and the evident meaning which the office girls attached to the work situation do again add to the point made earlier that the goals of the participants of an organisation are significant variables, and that theories of bureaucracy should not be too ready to assume in advance the meanings which participants attach to the situation as a consequence of bureaucracy. Nevertheless, what comes through strongly, and no doubt what Miss Coote wanted to stress, is the apparent lack of control which the subordinate at the lower end of the hierarchy has. The descriptions, an appendage to a machine or a mere cog in a big machine, seem valid in relation to this situation. It is at this stage that terms like rationalisation and routinisation, which we shall meet again later, and which can imply the search for efficiency and smoothness of operation when used from the point of view of the controllers of an organisation, can come to be equated with oppression and alienation from the point of view of the underdog.

WHOSE SIDE ARE WE ON?

This brings us to a very important point. Images of bureaucracy arise out of the values and concerns of their constructors. As we noted earlier, questions about bureaucracy are ultimately questions about power, and we can be interested in how to impose our will on others or how to stop others imposing their will on us. We could pretend to stand aside and just say that we are observers attempting to analyse how the process works, but almost inevitably we must take the side of the dominators or the dominated, because we cannot avoid in the end some kind of judgment about the outcome of the process. Clearly the image will be different then, according to whose side we are on. That, however, is not the end, because the construction of the image depends also on the process of interaction which leads the constructor to his image. As Howard Becker has pointed out, if we take the side of the subordinate and refuse to accept that 'truth' is the way that the highest members of a hierarchy see things, our access to information is restricted and the very credibility of the image is in doubt from the start.[11] Every image therefore, starts with an act of commitment which predisposes and tends to categorise the image.

Much, then, depends on the stage we are at in the socialisation process to which I referred in the introduction. Our commitments and our views of the world are in constant interaction with those of the people around us. In a hierarchy there is more than an equal chance that the views of those higher up in the hierarchy are likely to gain at least tacit acceptance among those lower down, especially if an effort is made through directed training to gain that acceptance. Since in a modern industrial society most of us are engaged in hierarchical situations, it is perhaps amazing that there are still varying images of bureaucracy. Why do we not all share a view which stresses the beneficence, smoothness and rationality of our bureaucracies? This, it seems, can only really adequately be explained in terms of the experienced contradictions which arise in the process of socialisation—the status dissonance of the college teachers, the call for participation which ends in ritualised and trivialised meetings, the differences between the theory and practice of teachers, the contrast between the claimed power of administrators and their cotton wool reaction to apparent failure of obligation. Many more have been alluded to, and most readers will immediately think of others. In addition, we must allow for the fact that man learns from such experiences that he can share in this contradictoriness. Through social action there is just a possibility that we can control rather than be controlled. The image of a new world can stir in us a desire for change, and with support the effort sometimes seems worth while. The blandishments of the present hierarchy, possible sharing of control, advance of status, future security, can be put aside when a new image appears. But we can never be certain, as Solzhenitsyn and Kafka have shown us.

WHOSE SIDE ARE WE MEANT TO BE ON?

The nature of Rusanov's work had been for many years, by now almost twenty, that of personnel records administration. It was a job that went by different names in different institutions, but the substance of it was always the same. Only ignoramuses and uninformed outsiders were unaware what subtle, meticulous work it was, what talent it required. It was a form of poetry not yet mastered by the poets themselves. As every man goes through life he fills in a number of forms for the record, each containing a number of questions. A man's answer to one question on one form becomes a little thread, permanently connecting him to the local centre of personnel records administration. There are thus hundreds of little threads radiating from every man, millions of threads in all. If these threads were suddenly to become visible, the whole sky would look like a spider's web, and if they materialised as elastic bands, buses, trams and even people would all lose the ability to move, and the wind would be unable to carry torn-up newspapers or autumn leaves along the streets of the city. They are not visible, they are not material, but every man is constantly aware of their existence. The point is that a so-called completely clean record was almost unattainable, an ideal, like absolute truth. Something negative or suspicious can always be noted down against any man alive. Everyone is guilty of something or has something to conceal. All one has to do is to look hard enough to find out what it is.

Each man, permanently aware of his own invisible threads, naturally develops a respect for the people who manipulate the threads, who manage personnel records administration, that most complicated science, and for these people's authority.[12]

How far we are enmeshed in Rusanov's dream world, of sub-servience to and control by an all pervasive system, so that the moment we set aside the goals which our bureaucracy makes possible, to seek a change, we can be picked up and restrained by 'law', is always a cause of uncertainty. If in addition the control is so centralised that we are prevented from knowing the intentions of the dominant coalition, the task may seem hopeless, as Kafka's 'K.' found out in his dealings with 'The Castle'.

K. has been appointed to be a Land Surveyor in a distant country, but finds that there is some dispute between 'The Castle' and the local village authorities, where he has been told to take up his job, over a bureaucratic error which led to his appointment. K. simply becomes a pawn in the dispute but because of having been given, early in his stay in the village, two official assistants, he has some cause to think he has the power to alter the course of the dispute. When he actually achieves an interview with a local official, he is already beginning to see the limits of his situation:

Direct intercourse with the authorities was not particularly difficult then, for well organised as they might be, all they did was to guard the distant and invisible masters, while K. fought for something vitally near to him for himself, and moreover, at least at the very beginning, on his own initiative, for he was the attacker; and besides he fought not only for himself, but clearly for other powers as well which he did not know, but in which, without infringing the regulations of the authorities, he was permitted to believe. But now by the fact that they had at once amply met his wishes in all unimportant matters— and hitherto only unimportant matters had come up—they had robbed him of the possibility of light and easy victories, and with that, of the satisfaction which must accompany them and the well-grounded confidence for further and greater struggles which must result from them. Instead, they let K. go anywhere he liked—of course only within the village—and thus pampered and enervated him, ruled out all possibility of conflict, and transported him to an unofficial, totally unrecognised, troubled, and alien existence. In this life it might easily happen if he were not on his guard, that one day or other, in spite of the amiability of the authorities and the scrupulous fulfilment of all his exaggeratedly light duties, he might— deceived by the apparent favour shown him—conduct himself so imprudently that he might get a fall; and the authorities, still ever mild and friendly, and as it were against their own will, but in the name of some public regulation unknown to him, might have to come and clear him out of the way . . . [13]

As Professor Bauman has said:

The lofty puissance of 'The Castle' is based on the total ignorance on the part of the others, and certainly of outsiders like 'K.' as to what its next moves are going to be. Until submitted to intelligibly articulated rules, 'The Castle' remains invincible. Anybody hoping to play with 'The Castle' a game based on reciprocal predictions will do better if he gives up in time his vain pretentions to control a field of whose structure he has no information whatsoever. A mono-polistic access to information concerning some field makes the monopolist invincible, at least in the limits of the field in question. [14]

Not only does a challenge to bureaucratic goals in this kind of situation seem to be vain, but commitment to a subordinate's image of bureaucracy might also be unwise. Fortunately, man's view of what is wise and what is rational to other men in the circumstances, does not always influence his actions.

THE MARXIAN IMAGE

One image of bureaucracy, drawn from a theory about society which consistently has given much impetus to the taking of the position of the underdog in modern society, should also be considered. This is the view of Karl Marx, whose social theories are at the basis of worldwide political movements, concerned with the reconstruction of societies, so that inequalities and injustices seen to arise in the dominant capitalist economies of the world can be removed. For Marx, bureaucracy was the alienation of public life, for everywhere the power of the state tended to be concentrated on behalf of the interests of capitalists in the hands of a bureaucratic elite, so that other interests were not represented.

> The bureaucracy has in its possession the affairs of the state, the spiritual being of society; it belongs to it as private property. The general spirit of bureaucracy is the official secret, the mystery. . . . Conducting the affairs of state in public, even political consciousness, thus appear to the bureaucracy as high treason against its mystery. Authority is thus the principle of its knowledge and the deification of authoritarianism is its credo. But within itself this spiritualism turns into a coarse materialism, the materialism of dumb obedience. . . . As far as the individual bureaucrat is concerned, the goals of the state become his private goals: a hunting for higher jobs and the making of a career. . . . Bureaucracy has, therefore, to make life as materialistic as possible. . . . Hence the bureaucrat must always behave towards the real state in a Jesuitical fashion, be it consciously or unconsciously. . . . The bureaucrat sees the world as a mere object to be managed by him. . . . The bureaucracy is the illusory state alongside the real state, it is the spiritualism of the state. Everything has, therefore, a double meaning: the real and the bureaucratic one.[15]

This comes from the early works of Karl Marx, where he was most concerned with the necessity to change society, in order that man could find his true human nature in the recognition of himself as the creator of social institutions and not as their slave. Bureaucrats and bureaucracy were just one of the instruments of man's enslavement, but from the above it is clear that they were considered to be a most pernicious one. Not only did the bureaucracy capture the 'affairs of state', but the participation of members of the state was prevented by the bureaucratic ideology defining the limits of what was political and claiming the untouchability of its authority. Marx, too, uses his method of drawing out contradictions, by opposing the sheer materialism of the bureaucrats' own goals to the claimed spirituality of their official purpose. A further point is that bureaucrats can impose a definition of the state in terms of its divinity which mystifies the 'real state' with its inequalities and its repressions of the working classes.

In other parts of his work, Marx clearly recognised the possibility of the bureaucratisation of other parts of social life, as well as the administration of the state. Educational institutions, industrial and commercial organisations and even local communal associations were all mentioned. The same process of the capture of control by small elites, the justification of that control with reference to ideology and the mystification of the 'real' structure of relationships would doubtless follow.[16] For the creation of a more just society, one of the first stages was the necessary demystification of such structures, by the tools of Marxist analysis, and this should be followed by the abolition of such agencies of mystification as the bureaucracies. This would be an example of the unification of theory and practice which is the cornerstone of the Marxist message. Men must understand and change society.

Some scholars have suggested that Marx did not stress enough the image of bureaucracy, and that it did not form such an important aspect of his later thinking. While others have contested this, it seems to be the case that twentieth-century Marxists have come into conflict over the question of bureaucracy, and Lichtheim notes that 'the dichotomy of bourgeoisie and proletariat (is) giving way to a new cleavage between the planners and the planned, or between bureaucrats and workers'.[17] The conflict has arisen and Marxist theories are changing as a result of the experience of great centralisation in socialist states and in socialist parties in Europe and elsewhere. An example of the analysis of this phenomenon is that by the Yugoslav writer Milovan Djilas, in his book *The New Class*, in which he poses many problems by suggesting that the communist party bureaucracy has taken on the form of a new class, supplanting the bourgeoisie, but in no way diminishing the alienation of the workers.[18] The seven-year prison sentence which Djilas was given after the publication of the book is just in one way indicative of the kind of conflict that exists between Marxists, but it is also indicative of the kind of problems that emerge as images arise and are tested at the junction of experience and ideas. Images of bureaucracy can be very emotive, since they are closely related to deeply contested issues of power and domination in societies.

SUMMARY

We are at the point where we can see that to deal with the concept of bureaucracy requires an undertaking of a very complex nature. As we think and write about it, we are involved in it. It is an object to be considered, but it is also a part of our subjective experience. Thus when we speak of images of bureaucracy, we must draw attention to the way they arise. They arise at the junction of experience with our ways of thinking about and organising that experience. This was the reason for looking at the College and trying to analyse it with reference to 'the interrelations over time of groups of people in social structures' in the attempt *to understand processes from interactions in structures*. This synthesis of experience and theory can then be shown to be related closely to the goals that we bring to a situation and the ones that we find it possible to achieve in that situation. Both in the discussion of the college and the secretary's routine, particularly, but also elsewhere, reference had been made to the importance that should be attached to the participants' goals and, in consequence, the way that they define the situation. Finally, we have noted the importance of commitment to a particular view-point in the synthesis, and the way this will be influenced by the process of socialisation, the contradictions that arise in this, the alternative views which may then attract us and the degree of influence that the agencies holding these views can exercise over us.

Now let us look at what some of the many sociologists have had to say about bureaucracy, remembering that they have to some extent been involved in this complex process. What are the consequences of involvement in the sociological enterprise for the study of bureaucracy?

Sociologists and bureaucracy 3

THE TWO SOCIOLOGIES

Nineteenth-century sociologists and social thinkers can be seen to have been caught up with the experience of industrial society and the attempt to capture the meaning for man of the changes taking place in economic and social arrangements. Sociologists have, therefore, always been concerned with the stream of historically produced and reproduced ideas about these changes. The Marxian criticism of industrial society, with an extract of which we concluded the last chapter, was just one part of this stream which, as a whole, has tended to be concerned with the problems posed by the increasing specialisation of man's economic activities, in the division of labour, the consequent apparent breakdown of old communities with their ties based in traditional beliefs about authority, and the emergence of new urban conditions in which an increasing gap appeared between wealthy owners and managers, and poor workers, based in new kinds of power relationships. Sociologists' commitments to the solution of these problems have varied, and this has become one of the causes of disagreement between them.

The consequences of involvement in the sociological enterprise for the study of bureaucracy are of course related to these disagreements between sociologists. We must therefore attempt briefly to give some of the basic reasons for the disagreements. Here it is useful and instructive to look at one of the most cogent and interesting discussions of the development of sociological thought and the reasons for conflicting theories about society as well as methods for examining the validity of these theories. Published in 1970, Alan Dawe's article, 'The two sociologies'[1] outlines the proposition that the present discipline of sociology has grown out of the conflict between two modes of thinking: 'There are, then, two sociologies: a sociology of social system and a sociology of social action. They are grounded in the diametrically opposed concerns with two central problems, those of order and control' (p. 214). Dawe sees these two problems as underlining different approaches because they are based in different social philosophies. As such they are linked with human concerns which arose particularly in the eighteenth and nineteenth centuries, though their origins can be traced much farther back than this.

ORDER AND SYSTEM

The problem of order is that of the way in which individual desires can be constrained so that society can exist and a continual war of all against all avoided. This is often termed the Hobbesian problem, as it was the concern of the seventeenth-century philosopher, Thomas Hobbes. He lived in a time of civil wars, and regarded the worst government as better than anarchy. In his major treatise, *The Leviathan* (a biblical monster, here referring to the state), he sought ways to justify the monarchy which he saw as being symbolic of the people agreeing to form a state, and to invest a certain person with the government of it, so opting for order rather than chaos. Many sociologists see their discipline taking shape as a consequence of a desire to restore a collective set of beliefs to guide society in the face of what was regarded as disorder following the French and early industrial revolutions. Dawe also sees that this rather conservative reaction to the perceived effects of the two revolutions, is also a counterblast to some of the ideas of the rationalist philosophers of the eighteenth century (the Age of Enlightenment), particularly those which formed the basis of movements to subvert traditional authorities and to question the foundations of community life. Sociology thus became very concerned because of this reaction with such concepts as authority,

35

the group, the sacred and the community, and underlying these, as Dawe explains, with the notion of external constraint on man's actions. The source of this constraint was believed to be society itself. The search for order thus led some sociologists to a doctrinal position (that is, one where initial value commitments colour the whole approaches to explaining man's actions and relationships), which set society over its participants and gave it the status of a reality of its own kind, greater than the sum of its parts. It was another idea of the Enlightenment, however, that of society as a harmoniously functioning system, which attracted such sociologists and led them to characterise the wholeness of society as a social system. The notion of order came to be embodied in the idea of a system of central values on which there was fundamental agreement and which provided the stability in the social system, a balance or equilibrium to which there was a constant strain to return when things went wrong. When things were in equilibrium, then all the parts or subsystems (the family system, the education system, the economic system, the religious system and so on) would be functioning harmoniously, and the individual members, through the division of labour, playing interdependent roles. In some ways Max Weber's discussion of the bureaucratic order, one of the classic formulations in sociology, dating from the beginning of the twentieth century, will be seen later to fall in line with this approach, for as he discussed bureaucracy in its pure or most rational form it assumes the nature of a self-perpetuating system which imposes meaning on man. In system sociology, indeed, man only seems to act in consequence of the way that he has been socialised to act and his socialisation is seen as a one way process in which man learns the expectations that are held for him by the system and are derived from the central value system. The general paradigm (the model used for explanation) of this process is that which Coulson and Riddell discuss and dismiss, namely.

CULTURE ⟶ SOCIAL LEARNING ⟶ INDIVIDUAL[2]

(Here culture and central value system can be equated.) All meaning is seen to derive from the culture.

CONTROL AND ACTION

The problem of control is seen by Dawe to derive from what several scholars define to have been the dominant objective of the whole Age of Enlightenment. The whole object of the rational, scientific enterprise which the Enlightenment philosophers encouraged was the solution of the problem of how human beings could regain control over the institutions and situations which man had essentially created, but which were up to that time largely defined as products of mystical and transcendental or supra human forces. Further the enterprise was concerned to replace the notion that the ideal future was in some way an imposition of divine meaning on the world and as such out of man's control, with the view that the gap between what 'is' and what 'ought to be', between the actual and the ideal, is an entirely human creation. 'In such a perspective, action constitutes an unceasing attempt to exert control over existing situations, relationships and institutions in such a way as to bring them into line with human constructions of their ideal meanings.'[3]

What has entered sociology is a language of social action directly related to the problem of control, starting from a concern with man's own subjective experiences and ideals and placing them in a historical process.

> The basic point is that the initial premises of subjectivity and historicity, in which that language is grounded, are implicit in the gap between the actual and the ideal; for the attempt to transcend the gap is essentially an attempt to impose ideal meanings on existing situations. Hence the linking concepts of meaning and action; the concepts of ends as desired future states, and of the existing situation as providing conditions to be transcended or overcome and means to be utilised; and the notion of actors defining their own situations and attempting to control them in terms of their definitions.[4]

The language has never become an integrated perspective in the way that the system perspective has. It enters significantly into the work of Max Weber and the early concerns of the American sociologist Talcott Parsons, but for these and others it tends to form a point of tension standing against the language of the organic system and within which it often seems to be in the end enclosed. Thus at times theoretically social action confronts the social system, and at others social action is consumed by the social system. For Dawe this is evidence of the fluctuating concerns of sociologists with the problem of control at one time and with the problem of order at another. Sociology is thus grounded in conflicts about values and commitment, and conflict infuses the whole of the attempts to build sociological theories and the methods used to gather evidence in order to validate such theories. In the case of methods the conflict can be seen in terms of the attempt based on systemic assumptions to rely on analysis using mathematical paradigms at one extreme, and at the other the attempt to give attention only to a close reading of the language of interaction situations. (Students should perhaps look at the variation in papers reporting empirical work in an established sociological journal and mark the contrasts of approach.[5])

VALUES AND MAX WEBER

This summary does not do complete justice to the depth of thought and analysis in Dawe's paper, but I have drawn from it the essential component for the case that is being argued here, and that is the essential value commitments of sociology and the ensuing impact of these on sociological studies. This Dawe carries further in another paper, 'The relevance of values' which he contributed to a series of papers to commemorate the fiftieth anniversary of the death of Max Weber, in 1970.[6] Using the critique developed in the previous paper and combining this with a close inspection of the work of Max Weber, he shows that modern sociology has been oversimplistic in interpreting Weber on the question of the value-neutrality of sociological analysis. As Wrong has said, too, Weber's

> insistence on the distinction between objective knowledge and the personal moral values of the knower. ... (has) ... earned Weber the reputation of being the foremost exponent of 'value-free social science', of a social science that is ethically and politically neutral

and eschews all concern with what ought to be in favour of concentrating on what is. The position has completely carried the day to the point of having become—at least until very recently—an unquestioned dogma of contemporary social science.[7]

Both Wrong and Dawe go on to make similar points that Weber's work is infused with value. Dawe notes, too, that what Weber meant by his statement about the distinction

> was that, within the limits of the inescapably one-sided viewpoint, it is both possible and necessary to validate one's substantive propositions. . . . For it is a necessary test of all forms of argument, be they sociological, ethical or whatever, that in so far as they incorporate propositions with an empirical content, those propositions shall be shown, by means of agreed criteria, to connect with the empirical world.[8]

Even this, of course, is not without problems, considering what has already been said about methods.

There is a further aspect of Weber's statement, which, Dawe shows, may have misled many of his successors, and that is that Weber was convinced of what he called 'disenchantment of the world', by the forces of science and bureaucracy. He hoped perhaps that he could stem the tide of rationalisation, and his plea for ethical neutrality can be seen as a challenge to the dominant, rationalising ethic of science. It is, therefore, an aspect of Weber's concern with the problem of control, a concern which cannot be in doubt when we read an extract from his famous speech on bureaucracy:

> Already now, throughout private enterprise in wholesale manufacture as well as in all other economic enterprises run on modern lines, rational calculation is manifest at every stage. By it, the performance of each individual worker is mathematically measured, each man becomes a little cog in the machine and, aware of this, his one preoccupation is whether he can become a bigger cog. It is . . . horrible to think that the world could one day be filled with nothing but those little cogs, little men clinging to little jobs and striving towards bigger ones. . . . This passion for bureaucracy, as we have

heard it expressed here, is enough to drive one to despair. It *is* . . . as if we were deliberately to become men who need order and nothing but order, who become nervous and cowardly if for one moment this order wavers, and helpless if they are torn away from their total incorporation in it. That the world should know no men but these: it is in such an evolution that we are already caught up, and the great question is, therefore, not how we can promote and hasten it, but what can we oppose to this machinery in order to keep a portion of mankind free from this parcelling-out of the soul, from this supreme mastery of the bureaucratic way of life.[9]

But, of course, Weber's plea for ethical neutrality was related to his own personal ethical imperatives which led him not only to regret bureaucracy, but also somewhat contradictorily to want to keep it. Note that he wants to oppose it, *only* 'to keep a portion of mankind free'.

Both as Dawe says and Gouldner elaborates[10], Weber was an ascetic Protestant who believed in individual autonomy, and the duty of all men to act 'responsibly'. He considered that a rational separation of functions was the way in which a faith could be preserved and action undertaken. Thus he argued for the separation of teaching from propagandising, of statement of fact from statements of value, and of academic life from political action. He placed the cohesion and autonomy of the university above the freedom to expound any social values, and in this value position we see an entirely different Weber; one who valued the rationally directed state as preserving order and the right of all men to remain as little cogs, but with the freedom to think and work privately and 'responsibly'. Hence his considerable concern with clarity of concepts, and methods of explanation in the social sciences, and his pervading interest with rationality and bureaucracy.

Thus we find in Weber evidence of contradictions such as we hinted at in the previous chapter. It will be interesting to consider his analysis of bureaucracy in this light. In the rest of this chapter reference will repeatedly be made to the three volumes of the recent translation of Weber's major but unfinished work, *Economy and Society, an outline of interpretive sociology.*[11] This is, as the editors of the work suggest, a work of enormous complexity, though designed merely as an introduction. It draws together analyses of structures and processes in a comparative manner, and is consistently challenging to some of the previously most influential social theories of the nineteenth century. Written at the beginning of the twentieth century, it is still in many ways relevant today.

THE FOUNDATIONS OF WEBER'S DISCUSSION OF BUREAUCRACY

For Weber, sociology begins in the attempt to understand and interpret social action, its causes and its consequences. His concern is with the attribution of meaning to action:

> We shall speak of action insofar as the acting individual attaches a subjective meaning to his behaviour—be it overt or covert, omission or acquiescence. Action is social insofar as its subjective meaning takes account of the behaviour of others and is thereby oriented in its course (i, 4).

The task, then, is first of all to achieve an interpretation of action, whether it be concrete individual action or the action of a collectivity of individuals on the one hand, or some 'scientifically formulated pure type' action on the other, that is *adequate on the level of meaning*. That is, it is necessary to examine the intended meaning of the action and place it in an understandable sequence of events. Secondly, the sociologist must check whether this plausible reconstruction of events captures enough of the forces involved to be recognisably a general explanation of similar events across time or space. If it does then it can be said to be *causally adequate*.

Weber then draws attention to the importance of not assuming that our generalising concepts have a reality outside that of the social world in which they were created. Collectivities such as states, associations, business corporations, churches and schools are created by a process of interaction among individuals, but it is important also to recognise that such collectivities have a meaning in the minds of individual persons, partly as of something actually existing, partly as something with normative authority ... Actors thus in part orient their action to them, and in this role, such ideas have a powerful, often decisive, causal influence on the course of action of real individuals (i, 14).

It is always important, says Weber, to keep on asking the question of how they came to be taken as realities and how they were constructed in terms of the ends of individuals and groups.

Thus generalising concepts must remain close to the empirical world in which they are founded and for which they are attempts to be interpretive. Such are Weber's *ideal types*, which have the following characteristics:

1. They lack fullness of concrete content.
2. They are relatively precisely defined in terms of the highest possible degree of adequacy on the level of meaning.
3. They are an abstraction from reality but an aid to understanding in that they will attempt to show how closely concrete historical phenomena can be subsumed under them.

Thus Weber uses ideal types which refer to *historically specific types* of action such as those involved in his studies of Calvinism, the Indian caste system, and modern western capitalism, and to more *generalised types* of action, one of which is his notion of bureaucratic action. His concern was to define these phenomena with as great a degree of clarity as possible (pure ideal types) so that they could perform their functions of formulating terminology, classifications and hypotheses for sociology.

Weber begins with a classification of types of social action. He sees four pure types:

1. Instrumentally rational action, which is determined by expectations as to the behaviour of objects in the environment and of other human beings, where the expectations are seen as conditions or means for the attainment of the actor's own rationally pursued and calculated ends.

2. Value rational action, determined by a conscious belief for its own sake in some ethical, aesthetic, religious or other form of behaviour—not concerned with prospects of success in an instrumental sense.
3. Affectual action, determined by the actor's specific likes, dislikes and emotions.
4. Traditional action, determined by habit.

Again, these somewhat abstract types are rarely seen in social life and Weber notes that much action overlaps more than one category. Thus traditional action may be justified in terms of ultimate values and instrumentally rational action may be affected by some value-laden choice of goals.

Social action presupposes another important category, that of *social relationships*, a term which is

> used to denote the behaviour of a plurality of actors insofar as, in its meaningful content, the action of each takes account of that of the others and is oriented in these terms. The social relationship thus consists entirely and exclusively in the existence of a probability that there will be a meaningful course of social action—irrespective for the time being of the basis of that probability (i, 26).

Weber then looks at the basis of this probability in values and customs, but notes the increasing tendency for social action to be geared towards the instrumentally rational type and for the social relationships to be consequently 'rationalised'.

This brings him to two of the dominant themes of his work. First is the *organisation* which is defined as a social relationship which is either closed or limits the entrance of outsiders and develops regulations for activity which are enforced by a chief, possibly with an administrative staff. Where the activities are continuously oriented towards some ends which are specified he refers to the existence of a *formal organisation*. An organisation implies the distribution of power and domination, which is the second theme. *Power* is defined in situationally specific terms. It is the probability that one actor within a social relationship will be in a position to carry out his own will despite resistance, regardless of the basis on which this probability rests. *Domination* is the probability that a comand with a given specific content will be obeyed by a given group of persons (i, 53).

These concepts form the basis of his discussion of types of organisation. The themes of organisation and domination are integrated in what can be termed the *rationalisation thesis*. As we noted earlier Weber had a concern with what he called the disenchantment of the world, because of the process of rationalisation which he held to be occurring, evidence for which he saw in the increasing number of formal organisations and the emergence of new forms of domination.

Up to this point it is clear that by placing such emphasis on meaning and action, Weber is responding to the kind of values which link him closely with the problem of control, as Dawe outlined it. He is concerned with the human agency in explaining social phenomena and at this analytical level is on his guard against the reification of his concepts. Generalising from historical situations should not allow the generalisations to lose their contact with the social process in which they arise. The state, the church, the school and the business corporation are not to be seen as things with an existence independent of man and the meaning he attaches to them. Often too, in the substantive analysis, the struggle for control assumes a central significance. With reference to the thesis of rationalisation in his discussion of the sociology of law, we note:

These rationalising tendencies were not part of an articulate and unambiguous policy on the part of the wielders of power, they were rather driven in this direction by the needs of their own rational administration, as, for instance, in the case of the administrative machinery of the Papacy, or by powerful interest groups with whom they were allied and to whom rationality in substantive law and procedure constituted an advantage, as, for instance, to the bourgeois class . . . of modern times (ii, 809).

Nevertheless, it is in the thesis of rationalisation that we can sense the beginnings of reification, for Weber begins to lose sight of one of his types of rational action. Value rationality seems to disappear and the question of 'whose rationality?' does not seem to arise. Thus in the same discussion about the rationalisation of the law, we can sense this shift:

> Juridical formalism enables the legal system to operate like a technically rational machine. Thus it guarantees to individuals and groups within the system a relative maximum of freedom, and greatly increases for them the possibility of predicting the legal consequences of their actions. Procedure becomes a specific type of pacified contest, bound to fixed and inviolable 'rules of the game' (ii, 811).

Here there is more than a hint of the other Weber whose concern was with the problem of order. However, the pendulum swings again, and we learn that:

> Formal justice guarantees their formal legal interests. But because of the unequal distribution of economic power, which the system of formal justice legalises, this very freedom must time and again produce consequences which are contrary to the substantive postulates of religious ethics or of political expediency (ii, 812).

Immediately prior to the discussion of bureaucracy, Weber considers the questions of domination and the way that a structure of power can emerge in a society. We have already noted that this is one of the essential aspects of a discussion of bureaucracy, and that it is one of his chief concerns. Again in a way that symbolises this whole consideration of Weber's approach, he says: 'In a great number of cases the emergence of rational association from amorphous social action has been due to domination and the way in which it has been exercised' (iii, 941). Or we might say, from action to order. And what interests him most in this discussion is how domination succeeds. There is however, a continuing swing of the pendulum, as it were.

He notes that there are several different types of domination and stresses the importance of the way in which it will differ according to the situation. Domination will be different in an erotic situation

45

from what it will be on the battle-front or on the rostrum of a lecture-hall. He then suggests that as well as numerous other types, there are two opposing ones:

1. Domination that depends upon one side possessing over-whelming resources or a monopoly situation.
2. Domination that depends on one side having authority. .

Again he is stressing pure types, for clearly whereas we might consider the power of a teacher to reside purely in his apparent authority, arising from the norms that reside in the traditions of education, we must also note that his power might lie in his apparent monopoly of knowledge. Weber stresses the pure types, in order to point to the weakness of, for instance, what he considered to be Marxist theory about power relations residing in the economic realm, and in order secondly to concentrate on the normative element in domination. The important question becomes, what makes the command acceptable as a valid norm, and as part of the answer he introduces a "psychological" paradigm to illustrate the link between command and compliance:

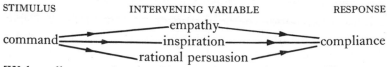

STIMULUS   INTERVENING VARIABLE   RESPONSE

command — empathy / inspiration / rational persuasion — compliance

[Weber allows a mixture of intervening variables as well]

but then adds:

> The performance of the command may have been motivated by the ruled's own conviction of its propriety, or by his sense of duty, or by fear, or by 'dull' custom, or by a desire to obtain some benefit for himself. *Sociologically, these differences are not necessarily relevant* .... the sociological character of domination will differ according to the basic differences in the major modes of legitimation (iii, 946–7). (italics mine)

This seems very much like a 'view from the bridge' rather than one which is prepared to take into account the meanings which all the participants attach to the situation. He does not completely ignore these participants, however, and particularly in his succeeding discussion of democracy shows how important it is to look at the social relationships from the point of view of all the actors.

Weber develops the thesis that in the modern state, bureaucratic forms of administration will be the typical way in which domination is achieved, but notes that other forms of administration are possible, especially where leaders act as, and are taken by subjects to be, 'servants'. Such a situation will occur in a *direct democracy*, which exists where it can be assumed that everybody is equally qualified to conduct public affairs, where the scope of the power of command is kept at a minimum and where the principles of rotation of office, office holding by the drawing of lots or short-term election, and control of administrative officers by a general assembly are preserved. Democratic administration occurs in organisations which:

1. have local or limited numbers of members,
2. preserve social equality among members,
3. maintain simple and stable administrative functions, and
4. do not elaborate methods of training for administration.

Democratic administration of this kind, however, is unstable, says Weber, because of the development of stratification. The control of the administration tends to fall into the hands of the 'notables', people who are usually identified by 'high income', not involved in too much 'labour', and a prestigious "style of life". Social prestige may vary so that the monopoly of the notables may change hands—from the elders, for instance, to the producers, or the owners of the means of production. Where monopolisation of control occurs in what is labelled a democracy, 'democratic administration' may become a battle-cry for the dispossessed— hence the formation of parties to struggle for control. Then direct democratic administration probably will be at an end, because of the tendency of the parties themselves to develop hierarchical structures in order to fight for control in an organised manner. The whole process is affected, it appears, by the problem of control at a substantive level, for if the size of the organisation or state increases (a factor that must also be explained with reference to human motivation) more and more conditions are cause for debate and conflict. Weber at this point makes use of the concept of alienation to evaluate the meaning which the 'dispossessed' might attach to the situation.

Thus here again the emphasis in Weber's discussion has swung back to interaction, in which individuals and groups pursue ends which are both instrumental and value-oriented. Organisations are structured through the way in which individuals and groups are involved in the continuation of or struggle for domination:

> The structure . . . is determined by the kind of relationship between master or masters and the apparatus (of administration), the kind of relationship of both to the ruled . . . and its specific way of distributing the powers of command (iii, 953).

This structure will always tend to have the form of the leaders and the led, with the leadership composed of the 'masters', those who lead but do not derive their power by grant from others, and the apparatus of administrators, but at this stage Weber does not make the assumption that such a structure will be permanent and unchangeable. Because of the struggle for control, there will be a continuing need for the leadership to justify itself. He points to attacks that exposed some forms of the justification (or legitimation) in the nineteenth century:

> In times in which the class situation has become unambiguously and openly visible to everyone as the factor determining every man's individual fate, that very myth of the highly privileged about everyone having deserved his particular lot has often become one of the most passionately hated objects of attack; one ought only to think of . . . the class struggle of our own time in which such myths and the claim of legitimate domination based upon it have been the target of the most powerful and most effective attacks (iii, 953–4).

Thus legitimation is a very active process, and it seems somewhat odd that Weber should have decided to classify types of domination not by the various processes by which legitimation takes place, but by the norms which the leadership appeals to, in the process. Odd that is, unless we remember again the pendulum.

Thus Weber's pure types of domination are classified as those based on (1) a belief in a system of rational rules; (2) a belief in tradition and (3) a belief in the charisma of an outstanding person. He does say that in the first case the rules might have to be imposed from above, but in the other cases there is no immediate reference to the way in which tradition and charisma may be constructed.

THE PURE TYPE OF BUREAUCRATIC ACTION

Each of these types of domination then forms the basis for a particular type of administration. Where a leadership appeals to a system of rational rules, then for Weber the most rational form of administration will be that of bureaucracy. The ideal-typical form thus appears to be based on norms rather than the interaction in which the norms might be constructed, and it seems reasonable to question whether this pure type reaches near to the criterion of adequacy on the level of meaning (see above, p. 41). As was also mentioned earlier, Weber leaves out any discussion of different forms of rational action and there seems quite clearly to be reference only to the instrumental rationality of the 'masters'. Thus we are given the six 'principles' of bureaucracy and the six 'principles' behind the position of the bureaucratic official (iii, 956-62).

The six principles of bureaucracy are:

1. There are fixed and official jurisdictional areas—ordered by rules, so that official duties are regular activities, based on the ends of the organisation.

2. There is a firmly ordered hierarchy providing for the supervision of lower offices by specified higher ones. Lower officials have the right of appeal as a counter-balance to the regulated

domination from above. Such offices are not ephemeral—they are fixed and then filled by successive incumbents.
3. The management of the office is based on written documents and a filing system—hence clerks to keep the files. The office should be distinct from the home of the official and the segregation of business and family interests is presupposed· for all members of the bureaucracy.
4. Each specialised position demands specific training.
5. Official business should not be a secondary activity, but should occupy the energies of the official full-time.
6. The rules of the bureaucracy demand relevant learning and expertise based in relevant academic disciplines (law, public administration and management studies).

The six principles behind the position of the official are

1. Office holding is a 'vocation', requiring a prescribed course of training, the passing of examinations to indicate quality, impersonality in the conduct of the office.
2. The official enjoys a social esteem in accordance with his rank in the hierarchy.
3. The official is appointed by a superior authority.
4. The official usually enjoys tenure (of office) for life.
5. Security is ensured for the official by the payment of a salary in accord with his status in the hierarchy (and a pension at the end of his service).
6. Career stages will characterise the official's life and he will expect to be moved from less well paid to better paid offices with time.

Weber's discussion of the position of the official includes some recognition of the variety of interpretations that might be put on office holding, in accordance with perceived conditions affecting that office, such as, for instance, the sheer market situation of the aspiring official—in a developing country as against an advanced industrial society, or, in relation to the numbers of applicants with similar qualifications. There is also some discussion of the problems of career blockage, but in general these are subordinated to the view of the normative character of bureaucratic action, i.e. the explanation no longer considers the importance of the purposive basis of such action.

THE ADVANCE OF BUREAUCRACY: WEBER'S VIEW OF ITS CAUSES

Weber felt that this pure type of bureaucracy was close to the many state bureaucracies which he had examined in his vast reading of history, as well as to the increasing number of public and private bureaucracies, of which he had contemporary evidence. It was not a new phenomenon related to the industrialisation of Europe and America. The increasing number of bureaucratic administrations was what concerned him, as we have already indicated, and he attributed the causes of this 'rationalisation' to

1. the development of a money economy,
2. the increasing size of states and organisations,
3. the impact of cultural, economic and technological developments, and
4. the technical superiority of bureaucracy over other forms of administration.

First, while bureaucracies have existed in non-money economies, for example ancient Egypt, the extensive employment of officials close to the control of states and organisations could only occur without threat to the 'masters' if money salaries were available for compensation of officials, and the officials were not in consequence tempted to appropriate bureaucratic property for their own ends. Weber agrees that salaries are not the only aspect encouraging commitment and preventing subversion, and in a comment on this we can see something of his view about the rigour of a bureaucracy:

> The relative optimum for the success and maintenance of a rigorous mechanisation of the bureaucratic apparatus is offered by an assured salary connected with the opportunity of a career that is not dependent

upon mere accident and arbitrariness. Taut discipline and control, which at the same time have consideration for the official's sense of honour, and the development of prestige sentiments of the status group as well as the possibility of public criticism, also work in the same direction (iii, 968).

Second, Weber sees that the growth in size of states and organisations is linked with the advance of bureaucracy, but growth may also be a product of bureaucratisation, and both in the end may be consequent on other factors.

Third, such other factors Weber can see in the growth of wealth and property, particularly in the amassing of these in corporations, so that the protection of property, the settling of large-scale conflicts over property, the distribution of benefits to those adversely affected by the distribution of wealth and conflicts over this, and the control of communications, all become foci for large-scale formal administration.

But he attributes decisive significance to the fourth cause. The sheer technical superiority of this form of administration, as Weber sees it, is the prime cause of its adoption in the modern world. At this point in the analysis he seems completely absorbed by its mechanical, legal, rational order:

> Precision, speed, unambiguity, knowledge of the files, continuity, discretion, unity, strict subordination, reduction of friction and of material and personal costs—these are raised to the optimum point in the strictly bureaucratic administration, and especially in its monocratic form (iii, 973).

Once more he indicates this propensity to move towards an analysis which puts the bureaucratic order beyond the control of man, and to leave behind his social action frame of reference.

As such, bureaucracy is seen to be closely allied with modern western capitalism.

> Bureaucracy develops the more perfectly, the more it is dehumanised —the more completely it succeeds in eliminating from official business love, hatred and all purely personal, irrational and emotional

elements which escape calculation. This is appraised as its special virtue by capitalism. . . . Bureaucracy offers the attitudes demanded by the external apparatus of modern culture in the most favourable combination (iii, 975).

It is this combination which produces the utter pessimism which, critics have sensed, lies in Weber's analysis and it is this which colours completely his assessment of the consequences of bureaucratisation.

WEBER'S DISCUSSION OF THE CONSEQUENCES OF BUREAUCRACY

The prime consequence is *alienation* not only in industrial and commercial enterprises, but in every formal organisation, including the university, where researchers and teachers will be just as much cut off from their means of production as workers in a factory. Secondly, bureaucratisation leads to a bastardised form of democracy, for, not only are the democratic mass parties bureaucratically organised, but this leads to a decline in the active share of the subjects in government and *'the levelling of the governed* in the face of the governing and bureaucratically articulated group, which in turn may occupy a quite autocratic position both in fact and form' (iii, 985). Thirdly, a bureaucratised system of administration becomes *practically indestructible*, to the extent that everyone becomes so dependent upon it and life would stop without it. Even revolutionary forces cannot bring about an entirely different form of authority and so the *coup d'état* becomes the only possible way of changing the 'masters'. Fourthly, an entrenched bureaucracy *can serve any interests*. It is possible for capitalist or socialist 'masters' to become even more remote, and for their policy to be completely subverted by the bureaucracy. As Weber says 'The power position of a fully developed bureaucracy is always great, under normal conditions overpowering. The political "master" always finds himself, vis-à-vis the trained official, in the position of the dilettante facing the expert' (iii, 991).

It is during this discussion of the consequences of bureaucratisation that a direct link occurs with the speech quoted above (pp. 39–40), in which Weber allowed his despair with bureaucracy to yield to a plea for action. There is another reference to the mechanistic model and the bureaucrat as a 'small cog' in the works (iii, 988). Weber becomes then to some extent consumed with pessimism in his analysis, but like many other men, there are occasions, both 'public' and 'private', when human optimism stirs within him. The pessimism can be translated, through humour and the challenge of an audience, into a battle-cry. (We have made reference to this in the previous chapter, in relation to a newspaper article by Jo Grimond.)

Weber's pessimism is not completely consuming in the analysis either, and he recognises in his discussion that where the 'masters' are willing to employ experts to check upon experts in the bureaucracy, and where strong representative governments pushed along by economic and other interest groups, exist, then there can be some control over the power of the bureaucracy. Much will depend on the extent to which the various groups have access to vital sources of information, and their power to use it. There is also here a hint that things will not be too bad for people like Weber, who, as we mentioned above, wanted some segregation of functions. For 'the complete depersonalisation of administrative management by bureaucracy and the rational systemisation of law' (iii, 998) enable a clear distinction to be drawn between the 'public' and the 'private', and it is possible that the whole of the pessimistic analysis is related to Weber's desire to support his own ethical preferences. By suggesting that bureaucracy can subvert extremism of the right or the left, he presumably hopes to take the sting out of their ideological tails, and at the same time, to provide a justification for his own liberalism. As Gouldner has said:

> Throughout his work, Weber's strategy is to safeguard the integrity and freedom of action of both the state, as the instrument of German national policy, and of the university, as the embodiment of a larger Western tradition of rationalism. He feared that the expression of political-value judgements in the university would provoke the state into censoring the university and would imperil its autonomy.[12]

If this is the case, then it seems that we are able to understand the contradictions which exist in both the methodology and theory of bureaucracy which Weber gave us.

His own personal view seems to leave it possible for all men to be autonomous within limits. The limits are imposed by a rationally ordered stable state, and so the autonomy consists in the choice between pursuing a career as a member of a bureaucracy, or in one of the professions close to the administration of the state, getting a job as a worker in one of the increasingly large corporations, becoming a teacher, an academic or a minister of religion, or perhaps finally, becoming a politician and seeking representative status as one of the rulers. There obviously would be other job choices, but these would be determined by the bureaucratic system. The whole would function successfully provided each member acted rationally in seeking to do his own job as his special skills and training determined, and remaining uninvolved in the work of others. This would require self-control on the one hand and explicit rules on the other.

Bureaucratic domination allows all this. But his personal experience taught Weber that such order in the end could only be at the price of not questioning the values of the system, and of overlooking the class structure and the loss of control by the majority of individuals over the state and its apparatus. The recognition, too, that political struggle both arising from class conflict and from status differences within the various bureaucracies shows evidence of the centrality of the problem of control, led him to question his view of order. His sociology suggests that he wanted both 'order' and 'control' and never was able to resolve the problem, except in a negative sense of accepting that bureaucracy was just as bad for everyone else. If the class structure was fossilised in the end, and revolution was not worth while, then at least a quiet life was possible and the only problems would be technological—that is, provided everyone was rational like Weber, and accepted their total alienation. This, possibly, is an over-simplistic statement of Weber's value position, but it is related to the evidence of his statements in *Economy and Society*. The point

55

which must be underlined again, however, is the way in which his value position infuses the discussion of bureaucracy.

A similar conclusion can be drawn from looking at Weber's discussion of charisma and the way in which it becomes routinised, that is, taken over and made into a traditional or a bureaucratic form of domination. There always seems to be a hope in Weber that a faith can be retained and that this will be renewed through charisma, but that reason will continue to operate as well, rendering bureaucracy inevitable.

SUMMARY

It will be useful before we proceed to look at the way that Weber's model has entered into sociology since Weber, to summarise the points so far. First, in our concern to outline the basis of disagreements in sociology and the varying commitments of sociologists, we looked at the notion of the two sociologies and the important work of Alan Dawe. This suggested the formation of sociological concerns around two problems—the problem of order; how do we constrain individual desires so that society can exist and a continual chaos of wars and insurrections be avoided?—and the problem of control; how do individuals and groups control the human institutions which they have created? A sociology of social systems has developed using the language of the problem of order, and a sociology of social action has always potentially countered this, from concern with the problem of control. Sociology was thus seen as grounded in conflicts about values and commitment. The relevance of values was further considered with reference to the sociology of Max Weber, again through the interpretation of Alan Dawe, and the contradictions in Weber's foundations for the study of bureaucracy were noted. Weber was concerned both for 'order' and 'control' and an attempt was made to give some explanation of this in terms of his position of attempting to maintain both a rationalistic basis for his life and at the same time a basis in faith. We also looked at important Weberian categories such as social action, explanations which are adequate on the level of meaning, and causally adequate, ideal types, types of social action, social relationships, organisation, power, domination and legitimation, as well as considering the ideal types of direct democracy and bureaucracy. An attempt was made to draw attention to the contrasts between Weber's optimistic view of bureaucracy, and his pessimistic view of the bureaucratisation of society, as well as to show how his optimism seems to be related to his willingness to respond to the problem of order, and his pessimism, to the problem of control.

After Weber

Max Weber's discussion of bureaucracy has had a profound impact on all succeeding attempts to grapple with the complexities of modern industrial society. For him, of course, this discussion was integrated in his attempt to provide conceptual categories for the analysis of such societies and to fulfil what Professor Rex has called 'his overriding interest, namely the comparative study of the major historical social system'.[1] His complex value position, however, led him to elaborate categories which are more appropriate to a system sociology, based on the problem of order, in some cases, while in others, they are more appropriate to a sociology of social action, based on the problem of control. The ideal type of bureaucracy which he elaborated fits into the former set, while much of the discussion about it tends to suggest the need for a more action-oriented conceptual structure. This is very much at the heart of the reasons why there is a continuing debate with Weber, and why it is possible for Dawe to conclude his essay on 'The relevance of values' with the statement:

> Perhaps the real measure of the richness and significance of any body of work is that it retains the possibility of life through its susceptibility to interpretation and reinterpretation in the light of the concerns of successive generations. By that standard, Weber's work is still urgent and alive. Beyond this, however, its continuing vitality depends upon its unsurpassed statement of the sociological task. For Weber showed, contrary to everything that has since been said about his value theory, precisely how and why sociology *is* geared to that

ultimate question: 'what shall we do, and how shall we arrange our lives?'[2]

The debate has been at many levels, but mainly in modern sociology it has been at the level of theory and methods of analysing organisations, rather than at the level of industrial societies. Further, there has been a debate over semantics. Thus Albrow characterises the debate as follows:

It has two themes. The first is a dispute on the empirical validity (both historical and predictive) of his account of the nature and development of modern administration. The second, and more important, is a rejection of his association of the ideal type of bureaucracy with the concepts of rationality and efficiency.[3]

Albrow is more concerned with the second than the first, for it is the aim of his book to outline some of the problems concerned with attempting to define 'bureaucracy'. The semantic debate arises because sociologists have wanted to use Weber's categories but have not been able to assimilate his complex value position with their own. Albrow, attempting to take Weber's part in the debate, suggests that Weber would have rejected all the claims by sociologists that he had attempted to delineate the conditions for organisational efficiency and that by rationality he meant efficiency. He quotes most of the major figures of recent sociology who have concerned themselves with bureaucracy and modern administration as in some way being convinced that Weber's analysis of bureaucracy started with the equation, rationality equals efficiency. Robert Merton stresses the unintended consequences of bureaucratic organisation as a criticism of Weber.[4] Philip Selznick, after looking at the implications of the studies of organisations in America in the 1930s which stressed that informal relations played a major role in the working of an organisation, even to the extent of modifying the goals of the organisation,[5] felt that Weber had not paid enough attention to individuals and groups playing power politics within the organisation.[6] Talcott Parsons points to possible sources of inefficiency in Weber's administrative staff, because of the problems of role conflict of subordinates when faced with the incompatible expectations of technical experts, on the one hand, and administrative superiors, on the other, who did not possess as much technical expertise.[7] Reinhard Bendix suggests that the administrative efficiency aspect of Weber's ideal type will be to some extent mitigated by the variable application of social and political values by the bureaucrats.[8] Peter Blau says that:

> Weber's approach also implies that any deviation from the formal structure is detrimental to administrative efficiency. Since the ideal type is conceived as the perfectly efficient organisation, all differences from it must necessarily interfere with efficiency. There is considerable evidence that suggests the opposite conclusion.[9]

From his own evidence, he points particularly to the way that efficiency is the product of informal relations and turning a blind eye to official rules.

Albrow's stand-in defence of Weber, concentrates on stressing the varied ways in which Weber used 'rationality' and in particular that he was not only concerned with actual, or substantive, rationality in practice for achieving goals or ultimate values, but also with the way in which procedure in bureaucracy followed an orderly, regulated course; that is, formal rationality. He goes on:

> If we define efficiency in a reasonably conventional way as 'the attainment of a particular goal with the least possible detriment to other goals', we can see that it corresponds with none of Weber's categories of rationality. His idea of purposive rationality (Zweck-rationalitat—instrumental rationality) can be seen as comprising efficiency, but it was more than that, involving ends and means. The real relation between formal rationality and efficiency can best be understood by considering the means by which efficiency is commonly measured, through the calculation of cost in money terms, or in time, or energy expended. Such calculations are formal procedures which do not in themselves guarantee efficiency, but are among the conditions for determining what level of efficiency has been reached. At the heart of Weber's idea of formal rationality was the idea of correct calculation, in either numerical terms, as with the accountant, or in logical terms, as with the lawyer. This was normally a necessary though not sufficient condition for the attainment of goals; it could

even conflict with material rationality. Such an interpretation must
lead to the rejection of the charge levelled at Weber.[10]

But Albrow perhaps overlooks that there are elements in Weber's
discussion which allow anyone to assume the equation of rationality
with efficiency. The language which Weber uses in his discussion
of the advance of bureaucracy fairly glows with notions of the
high achievement of this form of administration (see above p. 52).
It will be remembered that we noted at this stage a clear propensity
to reify the concept of bureaucracy as a product of inevitable
external forces, denying control by man, so that its ends and those
of its 'masters' are assumed as given. In this way it is very easy
to assume that Weber's pure type of bureaucracy is meeting the
needs of the system. If, therefore, our 'anyone' is a sociologist
whose interests lie in theories starting from the systemic perspective, then Weber's ideal-type construct may well seem like an
attempt to build a model of an efficiently functioning administrative subsystem.

In addition, Albrow seems to accept the notion of Weber's
value-neutrality at this point and with it that he was attempting to
analyse only what happened when men believed in theories about
administrative rationality. We have already attempted to dispose
of the idea of value-neutrality, and so it seems possible to conclude
that both Weber's critics and Albrow are to some extent wrong,
in that both have underestimated the complexity of Weber's
position. Further, when Albrow out of his own preferences
indicates that the main theme of the debate with Weber was the
semantic one and leaves aside the other which he mentions,
namely the dispute about the empirical validity of Weber's
'account of the nature and development of modern administration', he seems to miss another stick with which to beat Weber's
critics. This would be in terms of the way that most of those
who have been concerned to correct what are regarded as
inadequacies in his theory of organisations, have completely
overlooked that his discussion of bureaucracy was very much part
of an integrated approach to the understanding of industrial

society, that bureaucratisation was defined in terms of the rationalisation of whole societies. Few sociologists have attempted to undertake to collect evidence starting from a coherent sociological framework so as to build up the sociology of a particular society. Talcott Parsons in his monumental work, *The Social System*, attempted from a structural-functionalist point of view to provide a theoretical framework for such studies, and used a scheme which in some ways derives from his studies of Max Weber, in that the characterisation of industrial society follows closely Weber's notion of a bureaucratised society. It depends so heavily on assumptions about consensus and integration, however, not to speak of its almost impenetrable jargon, that any value it might have for empirical study is largely lost.[11] Raymond Aron, who has derived much inspiration from Weber, also notes that he

> tries to reconstruct the whole of society, beginning with the relations between individuals; to establish economic, political and legal categories, so as to define the principal types of economic, political and legal structure; and finally to arrange the various relationships and structures he has distinguished in a historical sequence . . . (But, even so) we are still a long way from having a system of sociological concepts which would enable us to represent the whole of society with accuracy.[12]

That Weber has been taken as the classical starting point for many studies of organisations is obvious for all to see. Open the first pages of any set of readings on organisation theory, whether in a sociological setting or one of management studies, which hopes to provide a full cover, then Max Weber is usually the author of the first contribution.[13] This indicates the power of his categorisation of the administrative structure, as well as the strength of the tendency for more recent sociologists not to question too hard the social system, but to analyse its organisational parts.

THE SOCIOLOGY OF ORGANISATIONS

It will be impossible within the scope of this book to provide anything like a summary of work in the sociology of organisations, and in any case there are several which can suffice to provide adequate choice for students. Three are given here:

David Dunkerley, *The Study of Organizations*, Routledge & Kegan Paul, 1972. This provides a very useful, up to date summary at an introductory level, which covers a lot of ground and perhaps emphasises methods of study, rather than the theories behind them.

James G. March, ed., *Handbook of Organizations*, McNally, 1965. A huge compendium, covering foundations, methodology, theories and substantive areas. Though a little out-of-date now, still contains tremendous value.

David Silverman, *The Theory of Organizations; a sociological framework*, Heinemann, 1970. This is an attempt to examine the theoretical variety of contributions to the study of organisations. It links closely with the theoretical discussion of Alan Dawe, introduced at the beginning of chapter 3, in that Silverman finds weaknesses in approaches based in system theory and makes a case for the action frame of reference.

To maintain the continuity of the theme and to lay the foundations for the next development, it is necessary to look at the consequences of involvement in the contemporary sociological enterprise for the study of bureaucracy. We have already noted two important aspects of that, by referring to the two debates, the one about commitment in terms of Dawe's dichotomy, 'order' versus 'control' and the other, the debate with Weber. We noted too (p. 38), that the commitment of a sociologist infused the whole of his work, in both its theoretical and methodological aspects. So far we have concentrated on the discussion of Weber's work and the debates on the theoretical aspects rather than on the methodological ones. It is, of course, impossible to make a clear separation between theory and method, for they always interact with each other and with the underlying commitment; but in so far as *theory* concerns the development of concepts with which to tell plausible stories about aspects of the world of interaction and social relationships, that is, constructing sets of linked hypotheses which are attempts to find causal links between phenomena, and *method* is the use of various techniques to translate the hypotheses into testable propositions, to collect and analyse information from a defined universe of people and/or situations, or a sample of that universe, with reference to the propositions, and the attempt to assess the reliability and validity of the techniques and conclusions of analysis, then we can see some distinction. The distinction is often blurred by the extent to which sociologists maintain an approach which is as formal as is indicated by the above account. Often they do not. There is, however, in the sociology of organisations, a relatively clear line of separation between those who insist on the more formal approach and those who do not.

To some extent this line of separation corresponds with a distinction between those who prefer to keep theoretical discussion to a minimum and those for whom the theoretical discussion is really of greatest interest. But such a dichotomy overlooks the many pieces of work which do attempt to achieve a balance. A distinction is to be drawn, too, between those who use information from the universe or sample which is directly observable and can be taken as 'given', such as people's overt activities, their defined jobs or positions, 'official' statistics issued by an organisation and so on (*objective* information), and those who use information, which is gathered from people themselves in the form of statements or responses to questions, and which is meant to assess the meanings that they attach to situations (*subjective* information). Again the line of separation is blurred, and also information which starts by being subjective is sometimes so transformed by the analytical methods employed that it loses much of its subjectivity.

There is as fierce a debate about methodology as there is about theory in sociology. On the one hand there are those who are committed to the *social scientific* view, which for instance has been stated by a group of sociologists who have made a considerable contribution to the study of organisations, Pugh, Hickson and Hinings.[14] They recall the prescriptions for the development of sociology laid down by a group of American methodologists in what by now is a classical formulation, *Measurement and Prediction*.[15] There were three,

> the statement of theories in terms which permit the operationalisation of the concepts involved, and thus their verification or falsification; the isolation and description of the referents of the concepts, if possible by means of measurement; and rigorous tests of any theoretical propositions by means of controlled experiment and replication.[16]

This statement has links with the formal approach mentioned above, but it is important to stress that in the view of Pugh and his colleagues, such a formal method, should as far as possible use 'referents', or variables in the situation, which are capable of numerical transformation and measurement. This allows much more powerful mathematical procedures to be applied to the data, so that through mathematical theory it becomes possible to give some measure of central tendency or variation in the evidence drawn from the universe or sample with which they are concerned, and by further assumptions about the numerical transformations to examine the evidence for the existence of correlations and underlying factors among the variables. A strong pressure is thus exerted on sociologists to look for variables which are already easily quantifiable, and this tends to mean those of the objective kind, or to develop from those which are of a more subjective kind, number 'equivalents', which can be as crude as letting a response to a statement like 'I agree' equal 1 and 'I strongly agree' equal 2, and assuming the usual arithmetic relation between 1 and 2 in the rest of the analysis. But to be fair, there is usually much more sophistication to the selection of numerical equivalents than that. Also a whole string of careful procedures will be applied to make sure that nothing which is being claimed goes beyond the limits of what can be extracted from the evidence by the numerical analysis. In the end, therefore, the findings tend to be swallowed up by impressions of minimality, dictated by values placed on elegant research design, sophisticated analytical processes and use of computer time.

Some of the dimensions of the methodological debate will have already been apparent, in that the criticism levelled at the *scientific* view, that it strains the meaning of the evidence and to some extent prejudices the selection of variables, has been part of the debate. This other side of the debate arises from those who are concerned with subjectivity and historicity, and the feeling that the loss of meaning entailed in the mechanical transformation is too great to balance the gains that are claimed for the possibility of verification and replicability. Dawe, for instance, feels that a great deal can be gained by the careful application of the methods of literary criticism to statements and documents arising in organisations, which would give much more depth and subtlety to the analysis.[17] Cicourel adds further points in starting from an *ethnomethodological* position,[18] which stresses the importance of first recognising that man is a practical theorist himself, in that he imputes meanings to 'make sense' of the events of his world, and that the sociologist must, therefore, spend much time deciphering the common schemes of interpretation of man, in order to clarify how far they enter into his own 'academic' interpretations. These points have particular relevance to the complexity of interpreting bureaucracy, as well as to the debate we are considering:

> The structure of modern society reflects the rationalisation of everyday life via its bureaucratic institutions. The idealised goals of efficiency and rationality correspond to the logical-mathematical-physical view of the world; the filing systems and automation facilities of modern bureaucracies epitomise these goals. It is, therefore, no accident that the measurement systems used by sociologists receive their most intensive use when applied to data generated by modern bureaucracies. The very conditions for ordering and reporting the data of large-scale societal activities have built into them the assumptions which insure a quantitative product, irrespective of the structure

of the social acts originally observed and interpreted. The social conditions of our time provide a set of definitions—dictated primarily by considerations of efficiency and practicality—for bureaucratic officials to organise the experiences of their everyday work activities. ... Most of the data that sociologists honour as 'given', therefore, are largely the product of bureaucratically organised activities. ... The multitudinous perceptions and interpretations that went into the assembly of such data are invariably lost to the reader or user of such materials.[19]

One of the implications of this, and it has been implied throughout the discussion, is that the sociologist is an important variable in the research process.[20] Cicourel at a later stage incorporates this point in a set of prescriptions for the research process. It must

distinguish the researcher's rationalities as a scientific observer, the common sense meanings used by organisations and agency personnel for interpreting and classifying events into categories, and the actor's interpretive rules for making sense of his environment.[21]

On both sides of the debate methods of collecting and analysing data are defined as of great importance. Between there are many whose studies do not give quite so much attention to the methodological issues, but nevertheless they are valued for their contributions in other ways. At this stage it will be useful then to look closely at examples of work on bureaucracy related to organisations, keeping in mind the methodological debate. We will start with the work of Professor Pugh and his colleagues, and follow this with an examination of the work of Michel Crozier, whose *The Bureaucratic Phenomenon* does not pay great attention, at least in the text, to the methodological issues involved in his study of two bureaucratic organisations in France.[22] We shall defer to the next chapter, our consideration of the work of Professor Cicourel *The Educational Decision Makers*, since it forms an integral part of any study on bureaucracy and education[23] (see below pp. 92f).

SOCIAL SCIENTIFIC APPROACH TO BUREAUCRACY

Basically Professor Pugh and his colleagues start, as indicated above, in the prescriptions laid down by Stouffer and his colleagues, and having made the assumption that Weber's ideal type was meant to be applied to the structure of organisations, attempt to 'operationalise' the ideal type to test if indeed it is an adequate description of organisational structure. There is more to the enterprise than this, in that they recognise that there has been a continuing debate with Weber and a great deal of empirical research to take account of, which has in some ways modified the notion of organisational structure. Further, they are, therefore, interested in finding out whether any of the kind of hypotheses which Weber and others have put forward to explain organisational structure and bureaucratisation have any validity. They are particularly interested in the relation of size of organisation, technology used and certain environmental factors with organisational structure.

The rationale of their work is then first to pick up from the debate with Weber and the empirical research that bureaucracy consists of a number of characteristics, such as those Weber listed (see pp. 49–50 above). These characteristics are seen to vary, so that the word 'characteristics' is translated into 'dimensions', which then brings it into line with the possibility of mathematical measurement. A dimension can be assigned a value, and it is now a variable that can be entered into computational process. As they say:

> Measurement is central, and where relationships between objects can sensibly be expressed in terms of numbers, much more powerfully analytic operations can be performed. This is not to say that the development of scaling techniques in sociology is an easy task; the opposite is the case. But the effort is so rewarding in every way if it is made.[24]

We are left to imagine what the rewards might be.

During the process of defining and refining the dimensions of organisational structure or bureaucracy, their chief concern is to underline the concept of variability, not only because of the mathematical reason, but also because of the way that 'bureaucracy' has become so embedded in sociology that (a) the danger is that it will inhibit innovation ... and (b) remain as something inviolate'.[25] Yet they quote numerous cases where the concept has been redefined by the theorists, whom they seem in a way to be against, so that we may have to recognise that they have an ethical position which they feel in some way has to be protected. Yet they do not seem to want to make it altogether explicit. If pushed, they would probably want to say that they are looking for the characteristics of organisation that will promote technological innovation and growth in the economy.

The dimensions which they use for characterising organisational structure are:

Specialisation: the division of labour within the organisation, the distribution of official duties among a number of positions.

Standardisation: the extent to which procedures are governed by regulations.

Formalisation: the extent to which rules, procedures, instructions and communications are written.

Centralization: the locus of authority to make decisions affecting the organisation.

Configuration: the 'shape' of the role structure.[26]

There does not seem to be any significant departure here from Weber's ideal type, except perhaps to emphasise the variability, and so we may wonder again why they make noises about inhibition and inviolacy. Using these dimensions involves operationalising them, and this is achieved by designating in actual work situations actual indicators, in terms of overt activities, officially defined procedures and organisational charts—that is, in the main, organisationally defined *objective* variables—and using the indicators to derive a score on each dimension for each organisation studied.[27]

The next stage is then to examine the relationship between these structural variables, to see if there is any evidence that they all seem to be related. In other words, is there after all a common factor which runs through the organisation, which might then be called with justification, as a unitary idea, bureaucracy? The answer that comes through is not surprisingly 'No'. But it is interesting that there is, both in the initial test, comprising a study of forty-six organisations in the Birmingham area, and in the replication, comprising a study of nine organisations in Coventry, quite a high degree of interrelation between specialisation, standardisation and formalisation. Centralisation tends to be negatively correlated with these three, which the authors take to mean that the more organisations regulate more and more work activity, the more they decentralise. The problem here is to gauge whether that is what the mathematical analysis means. If we take just one of Cicourel's points, how do we know that it is not just an organisationally defined interrelation and not one to which actors in the situation attach any significance? This particularly becomes problematic when we note again the sources of their data.

The final stage comes when they take measures of the 'contextual' variables, like size, technology and environment, and relate these to the structural variables. Size is seen to be positively correlated with specialisation, standardisation and formalisation and negatively correlated with centralisation, and this leads to the somewhat ironic conclusion that 'the bigger the organisation, the more it is likely to bureaucratise'.[28] This is concluded, too, despite a very careful attempt to provide an empirically based classification of organisations and their structures which suggested that there were seven types of bureaucracy, two years prior to the publication of that statement.[29] At least it confirms most observations of the bureaucratic phenomenon, as in the case of the college in chapter 2. Technology is not so clearly related to structure. Environmental factors vary in their relationship to structure. A problem remains particularly in their inability to 'predict' clearly a structure which relates closely to technological innovation.

The authors, of course, claim in particular that their work indicates the complexity of social phenomena, and that there is a continuing need for more sophisticated approaches. Our general agreement would no doubt be voiced with that, and yet, if sophistication means more use of objective indicators, without the addition of at least some attempt to look at action and the way the actors define their situations, it would seem doubtful if we shall come any nearer to an understanding of the work of organisations as situations in which human beings interact. Indeed, this seems to be the general meaning of a recent paper by John Child,[30] which has examined a large number of organisational studies both in America and Britain, including the work of Pugh and his colleagues. It comes, too, from someone who has been attached very much to the social science movement, and argues that there has been a tendency to overlook completely the exercise of choice by decision-makers in such studies. He reminds us of the work of Burns and Stalker, which, though seeming to assume an approach that organisations would respond primarily to technological changes, placed great emphasis on the way that the intra-organisational political debate about goals, resources and decision-making power took place, in assigning an organisation into their mechanistic-organic typology.[31] He then introduces the concept of the 'dominant coalition' (see discussion of the college in chapter 2) and draws us back to the notions of power and bargaining between groups, which Weber and others have recognised as a key issue in understanding how an organisation is. For Child, too, it is in understanding the work of the "dominant coalition" that will help us to grasp hold of the reasons for technological innovation and growth.

CROZIER AND THE BUREAUCRATIC PHENOMENON

Power is one of the crucial elements of Crozier's discussion of bureaucracy, too, and this is not surprising since, although he starts his work with the intention of conducting a 'scientific study' and providing a 'clinical description', the analogy with the work of the previous school is not very strong (his method of collecting evidence is hardly discussed at all)[32] and the references to evidence are mainly in the form of summaries of actors' own remarks, concerning how they defined their work situation and the social relationships involved. His collection of evidence still

71

corresponds to good practice, however, in that it is designed to support an argument in which the contentions, based in his own theoretical standpoint, are made clear, and alternative explanations are considered. This does not intrude into the work, which is essentially meant to communicate and consider problems with a human content.

What Crozier calls the scientific approach is an enterprise based in the social system framework, which as we noted above (see pages 35f) starts with the assumption of a distinctive culture, a system of shared values which determines to a significant extent the patterns of interaction in any part of the social system. Hence the interactions which Crozier sees in the two organisations, a large clerical agency in Paris and a nationalised tobacco monopoly situated on three sites in the Parisian suburbs, are determined by French culture, and this he characterises briefly with reference to its emphasis on individuality and independence and the traditions of pre-revolutionary France. It is the existence of a rigidly controlled education system, socialising the children into these cultural traits, which maintains the continuity and determines in the future work force attitudes that he finds in the two organisations. The definitions of the work situation which he collects are cultural products, that is, they are in a sense given.

French culture is, however, facing a period of change, mainly because of external economic and technological changes, and this will particularly be experienced in economic organisations, but not evenly. Some organisations will hardly be affected by change (the Tobacco Monopoly), others a little and some a great deal. Thus organisations vary in relation to the degree of certainty or uncertainty they have about the environment. Uncertainty then becomes a crucial variable for him, for it links with basic French personality traits, in that the desire for individuality and independence can best be preserved by people maintaining as much uncertainty about themselves as possible. In other words, their power to control their situation depends on the degree to which they can prevent others eliminating uncertainty in their power to act.

Power . . . stems from the impossibility of eliminating uncertainty in the context of bounded rationality [a reference to a situational rationality, rather than some global view of rationality]. . . . The power of A over B depends on A's ability to predict B's behaviour and on the uncertainty of B about A's behaviour. As long as the requirements of action create situations of uncertainty, the individuals who have to face them have power over those who are affected by the results of their choice.[33]

So, in organisations, a power struggle emerges around every centre of uncertainty. It is in the interests of management, therefore, to ensure as much predictability as it can in its own work force, by hierarchical structuring, spreading organisational ideologies, and manipulating the flow of information or regulating access to it. It is just as much in the interests of members of the work force to use every available means to prevent this happening by restricting knowledge of their own skills and knowledge to outsiders.

But, says Crozier, the power struggle is not the only thing that arises out of French culture. There is a continuing need of consensus and cooperation in order to preserve the possibility of competition. Hence the tendency for individuals and groups to seek intragroup and intergroup relationships. This will explain the continuation of work-place norms, despite the power struggle.

Bureaucracy, which for Crozier is an extreme application of hierarchical structuring, centralising of decision-making and completely impersonal rules, will tend to occur most where almost all uncertainty has been removed, that is where environmental changes are likely to be small and the internal situation has over time become so well known to everyone in the organisation, or where uncertainty is considerable in terms of environmental changes. In the first case management will have successfully bureaucratised the system and will be almost the only ones to have some degree of uncertainty on their side. In the second case management will strive hard to create some certainty for themselves as against the environment, and the work force is likely to want to accede to this. Too much uncertainty is not a basis for achieving any goals. Bureaucracy is thus a pathological condition, for there is a tendency for centralisation and rule-making to become or to be taken as irreversible. Crozier remarks that 'a bureaucratic organisation is an organisation that cannot correct its behaviour by learning from its errors'.[34] It is also one that is characterized by "vicious circles" which have the following underlying pattern:

1. The rigidity of task definition, task arrangements, and the human relations network, results in a lack of communication with the environment and a lack of communications among the groups.
2. The resulting difficulties, instead of imposing a readjustment of the model, are utilised by individuals and groups for improving their position in the power struggle within the organisation.
3. Thus a new pressure is generated for impersonality and centralisation, the only solution to personal privileges.[35]

Change only comes to such organisations in a crisis or through some charismatic leader taking charge.

The problem of all this, which is an impressive discussion, is that it is based on the evidence of two organisations, only one of which was really thoroughly examined. The work on the Clerical Agency was more of a pilot study. The assumption of the cultural determination of the bureaucratic phenomenon is perhaps, therefore, not justified, although there is an attempt to relate the evidence of the organisation to documentary evidence about French institutions, in order to show similar bureaucratic tendencies. His book contains one of the few attempts to try to outline a description of a bureaucratised society. He does this, however, in order to make his value judgment on French society and to outline his own view of what should be.

> Now, when managerial planning for growth both in private and public organisations has definitely taken precedence over state and group attempts at controlling or regularising the blind forces of the market, when organisations come to recognise that it is better to allow a large tolerance for calculated waste and human deviances and

imperfections than to sacrifice growth to thrift and the pursuit of possible overlapping, waste and corruption, the rationale of the traditional system of organisation crumbles. The French bureaucratic system of organisation, as we have described and analysed it, cannot easily adjust to this new form of rationality. It is not fit for planning ahead, but for regularising, after the fact, the results of group struggles over the proposals of individuals. Planned growth implies greater trust in human motivations, fostering initiative at all levels, more cooperation between individuals, and more competition between groups.[36]

What he wants then is a new humanism to match the new rationalism. He thinks that this will come, but is not sure whether it will be born in the charisma of French youth, or in some external innovation which will impinge on France and its culture.

Crozier in holding this position overtly opposes, he claims, the conservatives who shroud themselves in nineteenth-century political economy and see bureaucracy as inevitable, and the revolutionaries, who seeing it inevitable in processes of democratic social action 'feel that a desperate gamble is the only hope'.[37] The problem is that his own theory which puts such great credence in the cultural origin of the bureaucratic phenomenon, itself takes away from man the ultimate power to forge his own destiny, and so he is only left with transcendental solutions, which would seem to place him in the conservative camp too.

In some respects, then, we can see a parallel between Crozier's account and that of the 'social scientists'. Both of them are concerned with 'predicting' what the new organisation with potentiality for innovation will be like, and see the problem lying with hardened, mechanistic and, in Crozier's sense, pathological bureaucracies, which tend towards a permanent and traditional existence. The ideology of technological innovation and growth forms the implicit basis, which maintains commitment to their enterprise. It is interesting to consider that the methodological differences between them in this respect have no significant consequences. There is a consequence, however, as will be clear, in terms of the extent to which the 'social' enters into the accounts.

For Crozier, the world of interaction and the attempt to communicate it in human terms has great significance. This at least gives us pause to think about both his categorisation of social thinkers into three groups, the conservatives, the revolutionaries and those like himself, and our tentative recategorisation of Crozier as conservative. His own categorisation is based on the tendencies of thinkers and writers to see the bureaucratisation of life as containing the inevitability of catastrophic paralysis—'a sort of Leviathan, preparing the enslavement of the human race'—a tendency which he sees arising from the kind of contradictory analysis, which we noted in Weber. He also attributes some of this to the analysis of Robert Michels and his famous aphorism, 'who says organisation, says oligarchy', derived from Michels's analysis of political parties at the beginning of the twentieth century. No doubt his own interpretation is based in a tension between this analysis and his own commitment to a view that bureaucracy is a pathology that can and must be rooted out. But this view of his is related to a hope for society that is ordered and, therefore, managed for flexible responses to innovation and change, so that uncertainty is not used for private or sectional ends. In this way, man is still not in control; he is still a robot organised by a system, guided by another culture. This concern for the problem of order is our reason for suggesting his underlying conservativeness.

Clearly, however, to leave it there would be an injustice to the whole analysis, which is born, not only out of a tension between pessimism and optimism, but also out of a tension between 'action' and 'system'. His account continually goes back to look at actors and their ends, and the strategies which they employ to achieve them. In this sense his work is very similar to that of Gouldner, which he admits.

Gouldner, in his *Patterns of Industrial Bureaucracy* draws attention to the weaknesses of systemic approaches, where 'the social scene described has sometimes been so completely stripped of people that the impression is unintentionally given that there are disembodied forces afoot, able to realise their ambitions apart from human action'.[38] His own approach is to look at and specify the goals of individuals and groups and to analyse organisations to the extent that they are based on consent between groups or imposition of a set of rules by one group on another. He suggests a typology of (a) *representative* and (b) *punishment-centred* bureaucracies as a result of the analysis of various theories and approaches. But in the end, his view and his underlying commitment are, like Crozier's, determined by the retention of a social system, based in modern technological innovation and growth. Bureaucracies might be questioned, not the social system. Since he wrote his work on bureaucracy, he has shifted towards the necessity for a different perspective in sociology, recognising its value position as an important aspect creating the kinds of questions it asks, and the methods it employs.[39]

As sociologists become more aware of themselves as a force in the analysis of the world, and as the recognition of man as actor grows, so the tendency to a theoretical approach which starts in 'action' and not in the 'system' will grow. The recognition of bureaucracy as imposed and of the struggles between groups who attach different meanings to their positions and work in bureaucratic situations, will lead us to an analysis which is more adequate on the level of meaning and to the understanding of the reference of bureaucratisation to the level of society, as Weber really intended.

In conclusion, it will be useful to specify the kind of analytical framework that would seem to be appropriate, given this tendency towards an action frame of reference, and assuming a commitment to the problem of control as outlined by Dawe. The analysis begins with the specification of individuals and groups involved in the situation under consideration, whether it be at the level of a society or an organisation in a society. These actors are then specified with reference to the way they act and interact with others in the context. Here descriptive categories will be used according to the context and the sociologist will tend to use labels that are communicated to him by the actors in that context. Next, is the stage of identifying the meanings that the actors attach to their action and interaction. The sociologist must at this stage develop hypotheses about meanings in terms of the goals which the actors hold, but the underlying assumption, which will add the sociologist's own commitment to the work, will enter here; that is the notion that the actor's attempts to make sense of his situation are related to his action to impose his own meanings on that situation and on the other actors who are involved with them, alternatively, the problem of control underlies and infuses the actors' meanings. Many sociologists might find it important to stop at this point, for the task of developing and testing hypotheses about meaning in interaction can be a consuming and important one. Others will want to go further, because of the knowledge in the form of hypotheses, evidence and opinions, which sociology has already accumulated. The essential tasks will be to unravel the processes by which the imposition of meanings leads to the creation and production of knowledge, skills, structures of social relationships and cultural values and artifacts, and the reproduction of these phenomena. It is at this level that the sociologist will begin to look at domination, legitimation and bureaucratisation as forms of production and reproduction related to control of societies and organisations, and at professionalisation, unionisation and privatisation (see below, p. 131) which are others, often associated with those who are seeking to attain control from other groups who are already defined as in control, or seeking to find alternative meanings where control seems impossible. There will also be other tasks such as those related to the analysis of production and reproduction where actors might be defined as not accepting the consequences of the dominant modes of production and reproduction. Such tasks should constantly link back with other stages in the process of framework building, particularly at the level of development of hypotheses about meaning. There must always be a recognition of the growth of new meanings, themselves grounded in the historical context of experience.

An attempt will be made to link this analytical form to the study of bureaucratisation and education, and bureaucratisation in contemporary Britain in the next two chapters.

SUMMARY

Having considered in the previous chapter the question of commitment in sociology through the discussion of Dawe's two sociologies, and the way that Weber's discussion of bureaucracy could be seen to be involved somewhat contradictorily in both, we have looked at the way in which succeeding sociological discussions of bureaucracy have been very much in the form of a debate with Weber which, as Albrow characterised it, was concerned with the validity of his account, and about the concepts of rationality and efficiency which Weber was seen to have used. We noted that it was to some extent because of the contradictions in Weber that it was possible to say that he was concerned with a model of administrative efficiency and that he was not being only involved in a discussion of the effects of legal-rational action in administration. Further, we looked at the contributions of some of the sociologists to the debate, and saw the general result as a sociology of organisations, rather than a serious attempt to develop a sociology of industrial societies, which had been part of Weber's major concerns. After this we considered, as one aspect of this debate in sociology the debate about methods, and the way in which a social scientific approach varies in its close association with mathematical theories, from other approaches, where methods less consciously intrude into the analysis. We also considered the implications of the ethnomethodological position, and the implication that the sociologist himself is a variable in the analysis. This led us to look at the work of Professors Pugh and Hickson as examples of a social scientific approach to the study of bureaucracy, and at the work of Michel Crozier and to a lesser extent Alvin Gouldner, for comparison and for indications of the move towards an analytical framework based in historicity and subjectivity, which seems appropriate for contemporary sociology. Such a framework was then outlined, based in the problem of control and concerned with meanings, production and reproduction.

Bureaucratisation and education 5

The choice of education as the first sphere for the discussion of bureaucratisation is related, first, to the author's own experience, as indicated in chapter 2, and secondly, to the generally recognised point that education, as it is at present formally organised, offers in small compass interestingly diverse situations where the individuals and groups involved are engaged in attempting to achieve a variety of ends. The recent tendency, too, for educational organisations, particularly in secondary and higher education, to be increased in size, (a) as a result of the movement for the common secondary school, avoiding the differentiation of pupils on the basis of measured ability at an early age, and (b) as a result of the decisions of governments in industrial states to spend vast sums of money on education for those over eighteen, has brought about the greater observability of educational administrators. Further, at a time when administrative work is becoming more obvious, students and teachers have become more conscious of, and have posed questions with more clarity about, who controls our schools, colleges and universities. In a sense, these have become zones of confrontation for the projects of administrators, teachers and students, producing new, or attempting to reproduce old, patterns of activity related to the question of control. The extent of questioning is indicated by the great increase in writing on education, in the number of official reports published about education in the last decade, the growth of studies in educational administration and a much more intensive debate about the 'role' of education in society.

EDUCATION AND THE STATE

This debate about the role of education is not new, and as far as the sociology of education is concerned, can be traced back to the work of Durkheim and Weber. The important aspect of this debate as far as we are concerned is the relation between the state and education. Both the 'state' and 'education' perhaps at this stage should be interpreted. By 'state' we are referring to what Weber called a monopolistic ruling organisation that claims compulsory control and attempts to maintain this control within a given area by the threatened or actual use of violence by agents and administrators.[1] Professor Miliband notes that this ruling organisation may consist of several elements, a government, a civil service, military and other agents of law enforcement, a judiciary, representative or parliamentary assemblies and local government. How far these elements are cohesive, how far one is dominant, and how far they are all independent of other groupings in the same territorial area or external to it, such as an economically dominant class or an imperialist state, remain empirical questions.[2] In this sense, the state is not a 'thing' independent of the interested actions of individuals and groups in a given territorial area, nor is it defined in terms of the sum total of political actions of all the members. By 'education' we are referring to the processes of teaching and learning, which are carried on in formally organised enterprises, usually labelled schools, colleges and universities.

The essential relation between education and the state was formed for Weber and Durkheim by the requirement that the orderly transmission of knowledge, skills and values in an industrial society should be controlled by an organisation that could be seen to be above sectional interests. The latter felt very strongly that the state should supervise

the influence exercised by adult generations on those that are not yet ready for social life ... [whose] object is to arouse and to develop in the child a certain number of physical, intellectual and moral states which are demanded of him both by the political society as a whole and the special milieu for which he is specifically destined.[3]

To leave this influence to private individuals and families would be to perpetuate inequalities and would not be in the national interest. For Durkheim, there was no necessity to discuss what the national interest might be, or how it might actually be maintained, except that teachers should be reminded constantly of the national sentiments and of their social function to maintain these. Above all the teachers had to inculcate 'respect for reason, for science, for ideas and sentiments which are at the base of democratic morality',[4] but there does not seem to have been a fear about the bureaucratic ways in which Durkheim's France was already pursuing his educational aims.

We have already seen much of Weber's thoughts about the importance of the state and his ambivalence about bureaucracy. This enters his discussion of education. On the one hand, the state can preserve the relative autonomy of educational institutions, and should do so in the interests of democracy. On the other hand, modern capitalist democracy demands bureaucratic administration and so 'educational institutions on the European continent, especially the institutions of higher learning . . . are dominated and influenced by the need for the kind of "education" which is bred by the system of specialised examinations or tests of expertise increasingly indispensable for modern bureaucracies'.[5] Whilst this reliance on examinations would get rid of aristocratic elites, it was doubtful whether the meritocracy by which they would be replaced would bring about any real democracy, and Weber recognises that the aspiration for elite status in this case would only serve to reinforce examination dominated education.

> If we hear from all sides demands for the introduction of regulated curricula culminating in specialised examinations, the reason behind this is, of course, not a suddenly awakened thirst for education, but rather the desire to limit the supply of candidates for these positions and to monopolise them for the holders of educational patents.[6]

Weber thus sees that not only does 'rationalisation' affect the bureaucratisation of the organisations of a state, but also involves the emergence of demands on education for adaptation to the goals of bureaucratic man.

Although there are times when bureaucratisation seems to be an irresistible force lying outside man's control, in Weber's analysis, he does remind us in the case of education, that there is a history of bureaucratisation. He notes that in an earlier day when elites sought legitimation through appeals to belief in tradition, the ideal of education was the cultivated man. Quality of life conduct was more sought after than specialised training. Now that forms of domination have changed, according to Weber, the ends of education have changed, but

> behind all the present discussions about the basic questions of the educational system there lurks decisively the struggle of the 'specialist' type of man against the older type of 'cultivated' man, a struggle conditioned by the irresistibly expanding bureaucratisation of all public and private relations of authority and by the ever increasing importance of experts and specialised knowledge.[7]

Here of course we come back to the problem of control, and it seems to be a reasonable proposition to draw from both Weber and Durkheim, that with state control of education, the form that education takes will be strongly influenced by the ideas of those who have achieved dominance in the state. If the ruling stratum or the dominant coalition make decisions which lead to the proliferation of bureaucratic structures of administration, then education will be used both to legitimate that set of structures and to select people for the hierarchies, provided that the dominant coalition share a belief in organised education in the first place, that is, it is part of a dominant ideology. Essentially, then, we must look at the process by which ruling groups emerge in a society, and the articulation of education with their ends of domination, if indeed it is relevant to them. We must not overlook the fact, too, that education may be caught up in a struggle between groups and that at times it may have more than one set of masters and more than one ideology affecting its own processes.[8] A further point of importance to be drawn from Weber's discussion, is that where education is seen to be important to dominant coalitions in a state, then educational organisations are likely to be linked firmly by the legal structure to the state, and so themselves come to be maintained by the same legal sanctions which support the state. Finally, we should not overlook another point, and that is the notion of the struggle between groups both to attain dominance in the state and in its educational organisations, implies the possibility that new meanings may be attached to education, and that people will use education in accordance with such meanings. To impose a pattern of education on members of a society does not necessitate that we should assume that they will always take that pattern and its assumed ends as given.

If Weber and Durkheim tend on the whole, to give the impression that education in capitalist society will support and reinforce the structures of that kind of society, with, perhaps, some opportunities for individuals who so require it to have a quiet life, away from the commitment to the 'rat-race', those who have adopted the Marxian analysis of capitalist society tend to be even more extreme in not seeming to allow anyone to escape its overwhelming forces. Education in such an analysis is totally alienating. One recent discussion of education from such a position is that of Istvan Meszaros.[9] Here, education is seen as the process through which people learn to take inside themselves

> the overall perspectives of commodity society as the unquestionable limits of their own aspirations. It is by doing so that the particular individuals 'contribute towards maintaining a conception of the world' (quoting Gramsci) and towards maintaining a specific form of social intercourse which corresponds to that conception of the world.

Thus people accept that education should reproduce the skills necessary for running the economy and the leadership groups and apparatus for political control, and, reflecting a remark of Weber,

> even in the field of higher education, which for a long time could shelter behind the glorified facade of its own irrelevance to the direct needs of a 'spontaneously' expanding 'laissez-faire' capitalism, the erstwhile ideal of creating a 'harmonious' and 'many-sided individual' has been gradually abandoned and the narrowest of specialisation prevailed in its place, feeding with 'advisers', 'experts'

and 'experts in expertise' the cancerously growing bureaucratic machinery of modern capitalism.

This is accompanied, too, by the

> disintegration of thought and knowledge into an increasing number of separate systems, more or less self-contained with its own language and recognising no responsibility for knowing or caring about what is going on across its frontiers (referring to a remark of Professor Jeffreys).[10]

The argument of Meszaros is thus to the effect that education serves the capitalist state not only in reproducing the individuals with the capacities to work for the state, but also with the commitment, because it will have carefully allowed them to accept the ruling ideology. Meanwhile, the mystification of the bureaucratisation process (see above pp. 30–1) is reproduced in segregating men from each other by function, and in creating the differentiated classification of knowledge, which becomes the basis for curricular specialisms. Thus far Weber would have gone, and indeed can be seen to have gone, though in less evocative language. Whereas, however, Weber in his pessimistic mood had no real theory of revolution, except through the emergence of charismatic persons, Meszaros has—drawing of course on the notion of contradictions. Continuing bureaucratisation will only increase the alienation of people, and the capitalist system, constantly having to legitimate itself, will continue to demand an expanding production of intellectuals by education. Such overproduction of intellectuals will lead to the multiplication of non-productive workers, which will lead to the weakening of the competitive position of the economy and eventually to its collapse. Education is likely to hasten the demand for change in other ways, particularly through the implementation of courses of education for leisure, which through stressing the creativity of leisure will open up a contradiction between it and the lack of creativity and human realisation in work. So education is in crisis, for it is at the same time demystifying the ideology of capitalism as well as maintaining it.

Thus education reproduces the capacities and commitments

required by the capitalist state, and at the same time produces the seeds by which it will be destroyed: 'The positive transcendence of alienation is, in the last analysis, an educational task, requiring a radical "cultural revolution" for its realisation.'[11] Such an analysis carries further that of Durkheim and Weber, and even if we do not accept the inevitability that the contradictions will be perceived, essentially the point is clear and that is the vital relation between the state and educational institutions. Processes going on in one are reflected in the other and will cause reactions in the other—there will be a dialectic between them. Also the notion of bureaucratisation enters into the analysis as one of the linking concepts, emphasising the structural relations between the two, through the segregating and separating which arises from the demands of specialisation, formalisation and standardisation.

At this stage, looking at the implications of classical theorising for our theme of bureaucratisation and education, it would seem that hypotheses must be developed in relation to the links between the state and education. There has in recent sociology of education been an almost unerring tendency to avoid drawing such links when discussing bureaucracy in education.

ORGANISATIONS AND EDUCATION

We have already noted the tendency for studies of bureaucracy to become studies of organisations. This has particularly been the case in American sociology, where commitment to the social system model presupposes that social units like schools, churches, hospitals, armies and corporations are parts of the social system functioning to maintain the whole in an orderly condition. Such social units are thus constructed and reconstructed to seek specific goals, which are given by the system. So far as schools as organisations are concerned the assumption is that, as Talcott Parsons in a very influential article has elaborated, they will be concerned to give children preparation for adult roles, by imparting to them both capacities and commitments.[12] In a sense, there is a similarity here with the analysis of Meszaros, but in the Parsonian model, there is not the same assumption of alienation and coercion requiring a cultural revolution in response. The goals arise from an underlying consensus. Because of this the central questions which are asked about schools are about the *effectiveness* in achieving the goals, and the *efficiency* with which they harness the resources at their disposal for goal achievement. This leads to assumptions about the schools' potency or impotency, in the case of the study of effectiveness, and despite the difficulties of coming to conclusions on the matter, the attempt goes on. One idiosyncratic author writing in this area has shown the futility of starting with assumptions about the goals of the school (even when they are said to be those of the teachers), by claiming the potency of schools in one volume and impotency in a second one. In the first, under the heading 'The rise of a new despotism' he writes:

> During the past hundred years there has grown up in our midst a new despotism: the rule of the teachers. Today they claim to decide what kind of people we shall be. This is not a joint and generally agreed decision even among the teachers themselves. One school has decided that Englishmen shall be decorous and self-restrained; another that they shall show greater spontaneity, even gaiety; a third that they shall be rooted in the ancient values of their locality; a fourth that they shall be 'universal men'. Curriculum, teaching methods and school organisation are shaped to achieve these ends. . . . Only those parents who are rich enough to buy their children out of the maintained schools are able to decide, in some measure, what their children shall become.[13]

In the second, under the heading of 'Impotent schools', he writes:

> Schools are underpowered in relation to the goals they try to attain. (In relation to the more ambitious societal goals which they are commonly set by politicians and the public—world peace, inter-racial harmony, the elimination of crime and economic abundance—they are chronically underpowered.) People more directly involved in schools set more modest and apparently realistic goals: the effective transmission of a body of knowledge, the promotion of physical, intellectual and artistic skills, the inculcation of sociomoral values and

attitudes, and the development of acceptable habits of behaviour. Neither teachers as individuals nor the arrangements within which they work are sufficiently powerful for more than modest success in these modest aims. Even the allegedly omnipotent 'total institution', to which some schools approximate, is most remarkable, on close scrutiny, for its ineptitude. The problem of contemporary education is to put more power into the system in order to overcome obstacles and resistances to the attainment of its goals.[14]

It is interesting that in the first extract, he argues from a starting point which does not assume consensus on goals for schools, and because of the assumed power of schools seems to be concerned that there might be some consensus. In the second, where schools at least are assumed to have some consensus, and a 'realistic' one at that, order is not being achieved, because the external system is not allocating sufficient resources for the work. His problems are dictated by the same model as Parsons elaborated.

Where the model leads to study of efficiency, the scholars then turn to questions about the adequacy of the various models of bureaucratic organisation. Corwin and Bidwell in the United States of America, and Banks and Swift in Britain, provide some of the more adequate summaries of the work done in this area.[15] Essentially, the Weberian ideal type is seen to be inadequate, for it overlooks the 'collegiality' of teachers and the variability of pupil involvement. ('Collegiality' was recognised by Weber as one of the ways in which bureaucracy could be limited; it refers to the tendency of teachers to act as professional equals despite differences of status and salary.) Other models or typologies, such as Gouldner's (see pp. 76–7) or that of Etzioni, are then considered. Etzioni, in fact, suggested the abandonment of the use of the notion of bureaucracy, entirely in favour of the concept of organisation, and built up a typology of organisations around the theoretical notion of the compliance relationship, based in the idea that elite members of organisations used different forms of power, while the lower participants adjusted to these with varying degrees of involvement.[16] At first it seems a good idea to classify organisations on the basis of compliance, since as we have noted several times, the ultimate questions will be about power, but Etzioni overlooks completely the kind of distribution of power which Crozier discussed, and in the end, what gains it might yield in the comparative analysis of complex organisations are likely to be lost in the considerable problems of deciding what kind of power and what kind of involvement are typical in particular organisations which have complex structures and involve social relationships of varying kinds. In addition there is a considerable bias built into the typology in favour of treating organisations as distinct systems, and not, therefore, asking questions about the links between organisations and the degree to which there is a dialectical relation between them and the legal framework of the state. The bias also extends to judging the 'stability' of the organisation as *the* normal criterion around which attempts by lower participants to make changes or to serve their own ends can be seen as abnormal or subversive, rather than assuming that the normal situation is one about which individuals and groups will have varying definitions.

As in other kinds of organisational studies, questions about efficiency of schools then tend to move to the implication for the schools of the sets of norms and values which tend to constrain interaction among the members. Often this boils down to four sets, those which arise in the organisation itself and constrain the interaction of teachers and pupils, those which act on the teachers as members of an occupation which they would like to have labelled a 'profession', those which act on the pupils as members of peer groups and those which arise in the community around the school and affect its relations with parents and the local education authority. These are sometimes defined as the school, the professional, the peer group and the community subcultures, indicating that they are subordinate to the wider culture of the social system in which the school and its community are placed. The identification of four subcultures is meant to suggest that members' definitions of situations in school might be variable, hence giving rise to some form of conflict, and that members themselves might find that they are torn between the norms of two or more subcultures, a situation usually termed role conflict.

An example of subcultural conflict might be that arising in a school in a middle-class suburb (social class is often taken to be the major variable explaining differences in community subcultures, though religious affiliation and race can be others) where parents on the whole are concerned with a view of society that stresses hierarchical arrangements and the goal of advancing up the hierarchy of statuses. In this view educational certificates, gained from passing examinations in recognisably separate areas of knowledge, are useful for pressing claims for higher status. Such a community subculture would clash with a school subculture which stressed the importance of integrated timetables, without the specification of separate subjects, of learning by project work, of the teacher being the problem-poser rather than the instructor and knowledge-giver and of treating examinations as problematic rather than central to the curriculum.[17] An example of role conflict might then be that experienced by a teacher in such a school as this, who recognises the expectations held for him by his headmaster and colleagues to support the school subculture, but also perceives that his own emergence from the working-class community of his youth was the result of much examination passing and that, therefore, the parents who continue to hold the necessity for such performances have also legitimate expectations of him as a teacher. To which set of expectations should he respond?[18]

Descriptions of this kind tend to start from assumptions about the existence of some kind of consensus, to justify the use of concepts like subculture and role, rather than treat such phenomena as themselves raising questions. One very important study did, however, treat the question of the existence of consensus as an empirical question, in relation to the concept of role. This was carried out by Neal Gross and his associates using a set of school superintendents, members of the school boards which controlled them and some of the teachers in their school systems, in Massachusetts, as the subjects for the research.[19] The research enterprise started from an examination of the language of role analysis, which suggested that there was a growing awareness of the weakness of the assumption of consensus behind the expectations held for people occupying positions in organisations. It was suggested that the concept 'role' should be defined for research purposes, as the set of expectations held for the incumbent of a position. Then it was noted that every incumbent of a particular position would have expectations held for him by people occupying several other positions. If these were arranged in some hierarchical order, as in most organisations, was it possible that there could be agreement on the whole set of expectations for all the activities of each incumbent of positions in such an organisation? The research which followed was mainly concerned with the position of the school superintendents and the expectations held for them, with reference to their performance in many areas such as appointment of teachers, policy-making for the school system, carrying out the directions of the school board, negotiating salaries for teachers and so on. The expectations of school board members and teachers were collected by various methods, including questionnaires and interviews, and the school superintendents who took part were subject to eight-hour-long interviews.

Apart from revealing an enormous amount of detail about the working of an American school system, the important conclusion to emerge was that rarely was there consensus in the expectations held for school superintendents and that they perceived incompatible expectations to be held for them. If consensus can only be defined as variable, and *not* an invariant condition existing behind social action, embedded in cultures and subcultures by agreement among the members of a social system, then it is not always an explanation of social action. Therefore, notions like culture or subculture and role only imply socially constructed ideas or images, to which some individuals and groups respond, and which sociologists may use only as variables. This finding clearly supports the idea that explanations should begin with the actors' own definitions of the situation, and links back to the whole argument for sociological analysis in terms of an action frame of reference. (It is of course one of the central pieces of evidence relating to the appropriateness of action sociology in Dawe's argument in 'The two sociologies'.)

Returning to the teacher we left with two incompatible sets of expectations: his own solution will be in terms of the meaning he attaches to the situation. Does he see the future in terms of a career in teaching and is this conflict in any way related to his future aspirations? Is he convinced that the 'progressive' methods used in the school are right in terms of ultimate values he holds about education? Is he caught up in team activity with other teachers pursuing such methods, or is he pursuing his teaching enterprise in his own classroom without much contact with the other teachers? Does his own experience with the children in his class leave him feeling unable to be an active architect of their ongoing experiences? Does he act in his classroom as he always feels he should? We cannot assume in advance the answers to such questions, nor be certain about the relevance of his previous experience, in terms of class background, his own education and membership of associations, to his present work. This is, however, where the sociologist must start if he is to build up typical pictures of teachers' action in school that are adequate on the level of meaning.

Such a start will not deny him the opportunity, to link the analysis with more generalised notions of action such as bureaucratisation and professionalisation, such as Cicourel and Kitsuse have done, in their study of counselling and guidance staff in a large American high school. (Here it will be useful to refer back to the previous chapter and the discussion about ethnomethodology, in which this work is based, see p. 66).

BUREAUCRATISATION AND PROFESSIONALISATION

In this work, Cicourel and Kitsuse, following their prescriptions for research by being concerned to isolate their own procedures for categorising their evidence, from those used by the personnel in the school whom they are studying, examine some general notions about the procedures used in the school and the ideologies that back them up, and the impact these have on the careers of high school students. In their methodology they were concerned to find out how counsellors, teachers and administrators in the school regarded their students and how they came to make routine decisions about them. This involved the use of interviews with standardised open-ended questions, and the tape-recording of the whole interview, so that full analysis of the language used was later possible. The responses were coded by a rough content analysis which evaluated a range of responses to the standardised questions and attempted to sort them into roughly equivalent groups. These groups related to the main variables they wanted to use to typify the actions of the various actors. It will be useful to itemise these:

(a) *Consellors and social workers at Lakeshore High School*
    1. extent of time commitment to the work at the school.
    2. views about the extent to which counselling is a specialised job.
    3. procedure in terms of rules for dealing with students.
    4. language used when dealing with student for defining him and his problem.
    5. extent of discussion of the case with others.
    6. method of recording the case and control of the files.

(Data for same set of variables was collected for another sample of counsellors from other schools, acting as a control group.)

(b) *Students at Lakeshore High School*
    1. evaluation of own school performance and influences leading to this.
    2. evaluation of parents' view of student's performance.
    3. choice of high school work programme and influences on this.
    4. the relation of this to choices for the future after leaving school.
    5. intentions with regard to going to college.
    6. extent of parental involvement in this.

(c) *Parents of Lakeshore High School students*
    1. evaluation of child's performance and influence on this.

93

2. parents' role in determining child's future.
3. extent of knowledge about college and relation of school programmes to these.
4. links between home and school.
5. information for allocation to a social class category.

In addition to this the researchers obtained information from the official records of the school, showing the ability and attainment scores of students and their allocation to college preparation and non-college courses within the school.[20]

Lakeshore High School, a large suburban high school, was chosen for the study because it had an unusually large group of counsellors, and it became possible to look at the way the decisions of this group related to the college-going intentions of the students, which were known in advance to be affected by the high academic reputation of the school, and parental pressure in the same direction. The students were largely drawn from middle-class homes.

The researchers were interested in three interrelated issues:

1. The effect of organisational sponsorship, through counselling, on the tendency for students to be selected for college preparation courses on the basis of social class rather than just on ability—a tendency reported in many previous researches in industrial societies.
2. The effect of the bureaucratisation of the counselling system and the professionalisation of its personnel on the definition and control of problematic students—the high and low achievers.
3. The possible future implications of these processes in counselling for narrowing down the range of choices left to students even from an early stage in their educational careers.

In the case of the first issue, the researchers found that there was a clear association between high social class and insertion in college preparation courses in the school, and that the chances for students of lower ability and attainment to be included in college preparation courses were much greater for those in the highest social class categories. The school offered theoretically free choice of courses programmes to students on entry, and so it might have been that the greater knowledge about college and the determination to press for college preparation courses among high social class parents and students accounted for this association. It was found, however, that there was a high degree of unrelatedness between parents' and students' intentions and the placement of students in college preparation courses, emphasised by a lack of knowledge about the implications of the school's courses among parents and students at the beginning of their courses and by a lack of activity designed to bring about insertion of students in college preparation courses by both parents and students either through talking about this or visiting the school with that purpose. Thus what has to be inferred is that school personnel sponsor some children and not others, and that they use ability and attainment test scores in conjunction with less codifiable information, such as judgments about appearances, probable parental wishes and the likelihood of support or otherwise for students at home and in school, when making decisions about the placement of students in college and non-college courses. In addition, the fact of placement and the limits which this will place on possible future performance in school will then be used to justify and reinforce these forms of organisational sponsorship. The researchers found considerable evidence of the working of such processes in the school through interviewing the counselling staff and discussing the manner in which they and teachers in the school shared information in labelling and placing students. The way that under- and over-achievers were dealt with was considered particularly crucial both for the students' future life chances and for indicating the character of the processes in which the school personnel were involved.

It is here that the study of the typical actions of personnel in school links with the study of more generalised processes, such as bureaucratisation and professionalisation. Cicourel and Kitsuse do not define what they mean explicitly by these processes, but it seems clear that for them the process of *bureaucratisation* involves the recognition of a skill, in the application of knowledge to a form of either production or service, as requiring some form of administrative control, so that attention is drawn to the appointment of personnel as specialists in the skill, to some form of standardisation of the application of the skill, and to the formalisation of procedure through the codification of rules either explicitly or implicity. As a process it involves negotiation possibly in an existing administrative system for the recognition of the specialism as a separate phenomenon and as having an identifiable organisational status. With this status the skill and the personnel applying it become part of a legal structure, so that sanctions can be used to back up expectations held for the work involved in return for the allocation of resources in the form of salaries or wages and various types of equipment. The process of *professionalisation* is the active claim for recognised competence in the performance of a skill, usually backed by claims about the importance of that skill in serving some societal or personal 'need', and depending on the specialised application of theory which can only be acquired through long training, by an occupational group, who thereby seek to gain an identifiably high and distinct status in a society. This implies that the term 'profession' is a label which is itself negotiable, and not something that is inevitably fixed. It is a symbol which members of occupations seek to have attached to them because of the relative advantages which are derived from it. Thus bureaucratisation and professionalisation obviously interpenetrate each other, in that one provides means for the other to take place, but bureaucratisation is a process seen as activated from above by those who are recognisably in control of a state or organisation within a state, for ordering and managing some enterprise, whilst professionalisation is activated from below, by agents wanting to be involved at as high a possible level as they can negotiate for themselves in the whole control process, in the state or organisation.

Thus, with regard to the second issue in their research, Cicourel and Kitsuse note that Lakeshore High School had through its administrators built up a department of counsellors to attempt to keep the administration in close touch with students, so that there could not be any official doubt that the school was allocating students to courses correctly, and that the individual talents of the students were matched to the kind of programme they were attempting. This is linked by the researchers to what they call the bureaucratisation of the search for talent throughout America, in consequence of the technological arms and equipment race with other advanced states, particularly the USSR after the shock of the sputnik. The counsellors themselves were at the same time engaged in establishing themselves, part of a national enterprise, both as legitimate practitioners and as indispensable to the schools. Where they were established it was on the basis of post-graduate qualifications in counselling and the performance of a coordinating role between 'unqualified' teachers and either the school administration or out-of-school special services operated by psychologists and social workers.

The consequences of both processes are identified in terms of the introduction of a language and a set of definitions of students and the control of crucial filing systems by the counsellors. From the interview material the researchers gathered that problem pupils tended to be defined in terms of a language that lay somewhere between the teacher type and the clinical type used by psychologists and others in external agencies. Instead of labelling pupils as simply 'lazy', 'indifferent', or 'unhappy at home' they moved towards terms which implied some kind of causal explanation used in professionally defined theories, such as 'rejected', 'overly dependent' or 'unresolved Oedipus problem'. This use of language not only defined student problems, but also justified the work of the counsellors to the teachers and administrators, or was perhaps an attempt to do so. The control of the records in the files was based on the overt claim by the counsellors that confidentiality was necessary to make meaningful links between counsellors and students possible, but the right to restrict access to the files was a further means of confirming their own organisational status. Both these strategies, the use of language and control of the files, might also be seen as the attempt to create areas of uncertainty which can be maintained and used, in Crozier's terms, in the organisational power struggle.

The consequences for the students in the school of these inter-penetrating processes are perhaps summed up best in the researchers' own words:[21]

> It is not that the so-called 'class-ascribed' character of student and parent aspirations are irrelevant for the outcome of the student's high school career. Rather the implementation of college-going aspirations is made problematic by the ways in which they are interpreted and reinterpreted by the professionals in a bureaucratically organized system . . . (p. 101) (Also) the . . . counselling system may provide adolescents with the motivations, the labels and the justifica-tions for a wide range of 'problems' . . . (p. 109) . . . [which] . . . tends to lead to a 'managed student' in all areas of his life, including his adjustment in school, at home, and with his peers, and his future educational aspirations and life plans (p. 122).

As for the future, Cicourel and Kitsuse conclude:

> The possibility of systematising the application of this principle of placement is now at hand. Advances in the theory and technology of computer systems provide techniques of processing large numbers of individuals on the basis of standardised units of information. Such units may contain objective as well as subjective information, facts as well as hearsay, rational as well as common-sense interpretations, thus giving due consideration to education not only as a science but also as an art. Insofar as the gathering, coding, and input of such information are bureaucratically controlled, it would be possible to specify the student's probable access to educational opportunities and future life chances by the processing of his cumulative records. In short, the contingencies of social mobility may be rationalised by the use of computer systems in the form of an actuarial table (pp. 141–2).

How far this prediction can be taken seriously, is a matter for debate, but the increasing control of vast and extremely costly technological equipment by professionals in state and private bureaucracies, in the interests of those bureaucracies, though ostensibly in the interests of individuals and groups they are serving, is to say the least problematic, since it becomes increasingly more difficult for individuals and groups to have much chance of being able to check upon the working of such processes, if they have any cause for doubting them. Much will depend upon the trust which the 'masters' can generate in the 'led' about the 'apparatus'. But doubt will always remain when members of the 'apparatus' or the 'masters' send shudders down our spines like the following:

> On the battlefield of the future, enemy forces will be located, trapped and targeted almost instantaneously through the use of data links, computer assisted intelligence evaluation and automated fire control ... I am confident the American people expect this country to take full advantage of its technology—to welcome and applaud the developments that will replace, wherever possible, the man with the machine.[22]

The methodology of Cicourel and Kitsuse stands in some contrast with that of the social scientific approach discussed in the last chapter, but despite its concentration on one case study, it approaches much more to the meanings of typical actors than the other. In addition, this study clearly establishes the links between the school as an organisation and the social context, with reference to social processes which are recognisably human in origin. Thus it breaks away from the tendency we criticised earlier in organisational studies which focus on intra-organisation processes as distinct from socially produced activity outside them. The emphasis here, by using the linking concepts of bureaucratisation and professionalisation, clearly puts the organisation in society. Further, the very important notion of the interpenetration of these two processes, and our attempt to draw out the implicit meanings of them with reference to Cicourel and Kitsuse's use, add another basis for constructing other hypotheses which parallels that inferred in the discussion of the state and education, earlier.

Much has been written about the interrelationship of the two processes,[23] but very often such analysis has started from rather reified notions about the distinctive characteristics of professional and bureaucratic work. Many sociologists have felt the necessity to discover how professionals might be able to work more effectively in an organisation, and in particular how they can resolve role conflicts which it is assumed will arise because of conflicting professional and bureaucratic expectations. It is important, however, to accept that actors' definition of their situations may make it impossible for the sociologist to distinguish between professional and bureaucratic orientations. To repeat what we concluded earlier, bureaucratisation and professionalisation are actively interpenetrating processes, in that one provides means for the other to take place. They are in a dialectical relationship such as we noted existed between the state and educational institutions.

Thus rather than abandon the notion of bureaucratisation, and leave sociology only with organisations and organisational processes, it seems appropriate to keep it, for it forms, as we have been suggesting, a very useful linking concept, showing the situations, in which people act according to a division of labour, to be genuinely part of the wider human society, even though it is broken into pieces by the power struggles and legitimating ideologies of various groups at times. Bureaucratisation brings to the notion of organisation the indication of imposed or negotiated administrative structures and of the possibilities for other forms of action such as professionalisation. To use organisation on its own tends to link sociological studies inevitably with the organic analogy, which in a sense mystifies the social structures with which we should be concerned.

Bureaucratisation conceptualises the process of penetration of everyday activities by the administrative structures activated by dominant coalitions, whether stable or changing, and it emphasises the means by which the decisions of the dominant coalitions are transmitted as definitions of the situation to actors in a society, the attempts to secure their compliance and the legal structure which can be used to sanction them for non-compliance.

ENGLISH EDUCATION

In many ways, English education has undergone a complex

bureaucratisation process, because the definitions of the situation, which have been and are being imposed on it, arise from several different but interrelated dominant coalitions, backed by the power of the state. These dominant coalitions lie in

(a) Central government, with the Department of Education and Science, headed by several ministers appointed by the Prime Minister from within his own political party and staffed by civil servants, mainly without experience other than civil service administration, and a small group of professionally recruited inspectors.[24]

(b) Local government, with nearly 150 county and county borough councils with their appointed education committees, each served by an education officer and permanent staff of officials and professional advisers.

(c) The universities, particularly the older collegiate and civil ones which are the seats of the academic dominant coalitions, maintaining the production and reproduction of knowledge, within and across subject boundaries, and providing the legitimacy for the examination boards through which the bureaucratisation of the hunt for talent in England is organised, and for most of the professions whose members graduate or are certificated in them, especially teaching.

(d) The churches, particularly the Anglican and Roman Catholic denominations, which through their national education committees and their diocesan committees and religious orders, exercise perhaps a waning influence, but still provide some of the capital, have some say in the management of about a quarter of the schools and colleges of education, particularly the independent and direct grant establishments, and have a lot of say in the syllabuses agreed for the teaching of religious education, which is the only compulsory subject in the English school curriculum.

The whole educational enterprise is controlled in a legal structure which derives its legitimacy from an Act of Parliament passed in

1944, so far as the education of children between the compulsory school attendance ages of five and sixteen is concerned. Statutory provision of compulsory education covers all but seven per cent of the children between these ages, the seven per cent being mainly in independent schools. There are also statutory instruments covering the financing of educational provision for those over sixteen in schools and colleges of further education, who are forming an increasing proportion of those in full-time education, and for higher education in universities, polytechnics and colleges of education. The annual cost of publicly financed education is of the order of £3000 million, of which the central government provides something over 60 per cent out of taxation, the local authorities providing the rest out of rates collected on properties owned and rented within their boundaries. This gives some indication of the relative power of the central government in relation to local authorities. They are, therefore, primarily agents of the central government, as far as the extent of overall provision and other aspects of education which can be directly costed are concerned. However, the legal structure which links the local authorities in this somewhat subordinate relationship to central government has not had a long history.

The first major education Act affecting English education was passed in 1870, and this was only intended, as a result of compromises between various groups on the extent of state intervention in what had up to then been regarded as a voluntary matter needing a little priming from state funds, to provide elementary education in the growing urban areas, where the churches or religious societies could not or would not provide it. The Act set up school boards to make such provision, but these were independent of existing local authorities, and often came into conflict with them and with the religious societies. There was no single central authority for educational provision until the end of the nineteenth century, funds being filtered through the often competing Education Department, Science and Art Department and the Charity Commission. The process of 'rationalisation' which led to the setting up of a central unified Board of Education in 1899, and the attachment of local responsibility for educational provision to the county and borough councils in the 1902 Act, has been described in various ways, but one description which perhaps captures most of all the conflict of meanings at the time concludes:

> The changes brought about in the educational system were ultimately the outcome of battles fought out amid much noise and dust. This is not a story of philanthropy and growing enlightenment resulting in a continuous upward curve of development but rather a history of breakthroughs and retreats, from which the lesson to emerge ... was that nothing is gained (or retained) without persistent and determined pressure.[25]

The battles continue and the legal structure is more the focus of negotiation than a definition of the situation which all have agreed upon. Clearly the battles centre round who should ultimately control the educational process and with what purposes in mind. Such conflicts have often been revealed by committees set up by central government to consider issues which as a result of determined pressure from one group or another have come to be 'public' issues. Thus in the taking of evidence by the Royal Commission on Local Government in England (the Maud Commission) in 1967, when the subject of a smaller number of larger local education authorities was being discussed, the members clearly had in mind the relevance of this conflict. The then permanent under-secretary (chief civil servant) at the Department of Education and Science, Sir Herbert Andrew, wanted to make quite sure that the members of the commission clearly understood that the Department accepted the principle of the local power of defiance, and went further, pointing out that in his experience 'most of the developments in the education system had come from one local authority or another; they do not emerge from Curzon Street and get imposed upon the system'.[26] Yet there are many in local authorities who are quite sure that this imposition potentiality exists, and see in the new local government reorganisation which has followed the Maud Report, though not in every way being consequent on its recommendations, an attempt by the Central Government to reduce local initiative.

Members of local authorities through their various national coordinating bodies have continually voiced their protests. The members of the National Association of Divisional Executives for Education, for instance, have gone on record as agreeing that their abolition by the new legislation is entirely detrimental to local control and that their claim for the principle of decentralisation cannot now be met.

> There are only three ways under the Bill in which such decentralisation can be effected. One is by the delegation of powers to officers in charge of an area of the new county. This is sheer bureaucracy—the officer, under guidance from the authority, determining local policy and its application.[27]

The other two ways seem to them equally bad. The image of bureaucracy has been used as we have seen too by others who have felt their lack of control over the educational organisations of which they are part, and this has constantly been rebutted by Ministers[28] as well as the permanent officials. Sir Herbert Andrew, again, replying to questions by members of the Select Committee of the House of Commons on Education and Science, when discussing teacher training stated:

> There is no central governing body determining the standardised production of a trained teacher through a carefully costed, uniform system. There is a great variety of arrangements which have grown up historically, but which some people think are valuable. There is no central organisation, omniscient and omnipotent, determining what happens at any point.[29]

There is however a continuing attempt by one group or another to impose its definitions of the situation on others, and there must be times when the members of Department of Education and Science wish that local authorities did not exist to complicate matters for them, for instance when in 1965 a Labour Government requested them to turn their secondary school systems into comprehensive forms, and when in 1971 a Conservative Government required them to stop giving free milk to children between seven and eleven in primary schools. In both these cases local authorities, usually though not completely so, controlled by the other major political party from that in office at Westminster, have used delaying tactics or have just refused to comply, to the extent that in the case of comprehensive reorganisation the request was withdrawn by the succeeding Conservative Government, in 1970.

The point is that bureaucratisation has not been, in English education at least, brought about by one dominant coalition, but has been made possible, I suggest, by the tendency for administrators in central and local government to develop means of finding defences against loss of powers, by being relatively secretive and by developing forms of relationships with the politicians on the one hand and the public on the other (especially their employees in the schools and colleges), which narrow down the possibility for private troubles to become public issues. The hierarchical form of administration suits admirably a situation in which control of information is seen to be a valuable good. It has further been made possible by the tendencies of teachers to seek professional status and to settle for salary scales which have increasingly emphasised a hierarchical arrangement of teacher status in the schools. (It has always been in the interest of education authorities, local and central, to have more than one salary scale for teachers, so that it is possible to control costs of teaching by having agreed proportions of teachers on different scales and attempting to maintain as far as possible the majority of salaries in the lower scales, something that is made easier by the high rate of replacement that occurs among young women teachers.)

In other words, the problems posed by the question of control in English education are eased by bureaucratisation, which maintains links across the organisations involved—the Department of Education and Science, the local education authorities, and the schools and colleges—but also, through the development of internal hierarchies, tends to keep separate to some extent these same organisations, for the minimum number of members will be involved in more than rudimentary concern for links between the organisations, and the majority on internally defined issues.

The whole bureaucratic process, with its battles, hides to some extent the existence of another set of conflicts concerning the purposes of education. Broadly three major meanings are attached to the process.[30]

1. That education should give all children an objective and fair means for obtaining work when they are adults. This view seems to be held by large sections of the population. Its counterpart as held by some occupying positions in dominant coalitions in the economic sphere is that it should meet the needs for educated manpower, by developing all the talents that exist in the population.
2. That education should lead to the increase of human knowledge. This view is particularly supported in the universities, where some hold the view that an elite of scientists and scholars should constantly have this purpose. It has a counterpart in a view which sees education as important in giving individuals the knowledge to enjoy their leisure in creative ways.
3. That education should have a social purpose, in implanting values in the young. This view has conservative and radical dimensions. The conservative view would tend toward the idea of maintaining traditional elite culture, and the radical view would be concerned with the awakening of consciousness of humanity, the critical awareness of presentday society and the creation of a more open classless society.

Provision of education by the state, through its local authorities, has never, because of the way that the bureaucratic process is linked to the structure of social relations in England, answered the demands of those who have claimed that it should serve the interests of all the population fairly, and who, through lack of private wealth, have been dependent on the collective action of the state. Thus when the organised working-class movement of the late nineteenth century claimed that elementary education provided the working class with no opportunity whatever for free mobility through the occupational status hierarchy, and that secondary education, reserved at the time for upper and middle class fee-payers, should become available to all, attempts to do something about this foundered in the prejudices built into the class structure of social relationships backed by the bureaucratic process. For instance, some school boards attempted to provide, through 'higher grade' elementary schools, an answer to such demands, but in the end these attempts were foiled, by recourse of the central government and its allies to the legal process: in what could have been a nicely stage-managed affair, the Cockerton judgment (1899–1901), ruled such schools illegal. This set the stage too, for the elimination of the school boards, which had come to be seen by some as the 'citadels of radicalism'.[31]

There has never been agreement about the purposes of education, since education has always closely reflected the constraints imposed on action by the class biases which have been reproduced in the structure of social relations in England. The demand of 'secondary education for all' has constantly been on the agenda of Labour Party conferences since at least 1918, but despite active encouragement of the idea through the 1920s, it only slowly came to be an item of national policy. Even then, through the conflicts within the bureaucratic process and the possibilities for obstruction or alternative interpretations of the notion, so as to reflect the interests of people within the various dominant coalitions, the eventual pattern of state secondary education for all which emerged, consisted largely of two types of school—the 'grammar' schools and the 'modern' schools. Though much was made of the 'parity of esteem', in fact the distinctions between them have always been fairly clear, in that, rather than reflecting the division of children on grounds of ability and potential attainment, they, as in the case of the Lakeshore High School, have always reflected the way in which the notions of ability and potential attainment have been interpreted within the educational organisations. Thus grammar schools tended to have a population over-representative of the middle classes, and the modern schools, of the working classes.[32] Further, of course, the competition for access to the secondary schools came to dominate the primary schools, which enabled a bureaucratisation of the large primary schools, at least, through streaming the pupils, differentiating the teachers and formalising the preparation for the selection procedure,[33] without much penetration, however, of administration personnel—these remained strictly in their offices in the City or County Hall, keeping their distance, but implicitly involved.

The 'success' of secondary school divisiveness was clearly publicised in a stream of official reports, which appeared in the late 1950s and 1960s, as radical pressure grew to attempt a renegotiation of the policy for secondary education. These reports showed the underlying social effects of education were not at all those which the radical view held that they should be. In other words, the consequences of bureaucratisation were in the continued dominance of the middle classes in a society which had politically declared itself to be wanting to remove the supposed basis of this class differentiation, through education.

Consequent attempts to refashion secondary education in a 'comprehensive' mode—by getting rid of the division between 'grammar' and 'modern' schools—have been similarly obstructed.[34] A Labour Government, after declaring itself at the time of the 1964 election to be intent on bringing about comprehensive reorganisation, was unable to do any more than issue a circular to authorities 'requesting' that they adopt comprehensive reorganisation, rather than 'requiring' them to do so. That the government was permissive rather than mandatory, was explained by the then Secretary of State, Anthony Crosland, as primarily a result of the lack of funds for new school building and the legacy of existing buildings—both a product of previous decisions and recommendations within the bureaucratic process in Whitehall and the Department of Education and Science in particular.[35] Similarly, the attempt to absorb the English independent secondary schools, catering by and large for the interests of richer middle-class parents in obtaining privileged starts in the transition form school to work, for their children (though these schools are not without some innovatory and erstwhile 'radical' intentions) was also nullified in the bureaucratic process.[36] The Public Schools Commission which was set up, found it impossible to reach agreement on proposals for their absorption, and nothing has been done to remove the social divisiveness which the Commission's Report showed.[37]

Even where local authorities accepted the request to 'go comprehensive' there were other forces in the bureaucratic process, based in the separation of education office and school spheres of influence, which led to outcomes not intended by those who held a radical purpose to be the intent of the common secondary school. The education office provided the school with buildings and equipment, but by the 'rules of the game' the teachers were left to manage the process of education. This meant, especially in cases where a grammar and a modern school were brought together, that by streaming the pupils, and using the same preparation routines for examinations as before the integration, little obvious change was produced in the distribution of qualifications and instead there was merely a reproduction of existing social relations.

It would be possible to show that the same kinds of consequences of bureaucratisation are apparent in the higher education sector. With the dominant coalitions, operating somewhat autonomously, in the universities able to stand quite firmly against other dominant coalitions, the outcome of the present 'binary' system of higher education is, again, the reproduction, even if in a somewhat elevated form, of the façade of social divisiveness. Some of the universities have become huge enterprises in which administration now forms a large and very obvious sphere for bureaucratisation and professionalisation. Such tendencies may well become the basis for some obstruction or at least prolonged negotiation if the dominant coalitions elsewhere attempt to operate the idea of comprehensive reorganisation in higher education.

We can conclude from this that bureaucratisation in English education is a response to conflict between dominant coalitions, and that its consequences are in the tendency for staff in organisations within the whole field to use the bureaucratic process for ends like professionalisation, while attempts to reach out for new goals tend to be obstructed or reinterpreted so that what possibilities might have existed for pupils and students are not realised. The process is dominated by the meanings which people attach to the existing structure of social relations in England. This is not to say that bureaucratisation is inevitable, and that changes cannot be brought about. The problem is that bureaucratisation tends to solve some of the conflicts between groups and to encourage commitment to its consequences among the sizeable number who are offered the security of careers. When others then pose questions about their lack of control or lack of security, their tendency to feel manipulated or managed, there is not much desire to generate the extra steam that might be required to alter the pace or to cope with the new kind of conflicts that might arise. Perhaps, however, in the events of 1968 and later in educational institutions throughout the world, there is an indication that bureaucratised education is creating the conditions in which the emergence of a counterculture becomes a possibility among the young.

SUMMARY .

In this chapter, we have looked at the question of bureaucratisation and education. We began by looking at some of the classical views in sociology about the state and education, taking note of the importance which Durkheim and Weber attached to the links. An instance of a Marxist type of analysis, using the work of Meszaros was also considered, from which we drew the conclusion that it is important to conceive a dialectical relation between education and the society in which it takes place. We then noted that it was in the study of education through organisation theory, with its prime questions concerning effectiveness and efficiency, that one of the most crucial studies leading to the understanding of the inadequacy of the structural-functionalist analysis had been produced—the work of Gross, Mason and McEachern. From this we moved to consider the case of Lakeshore High School, and the research of Cicourel and Kitsuse, which is both suggestive of an alternative framework for the study of an organisation using an ethnomethodological approach, and shows how the reciprocal links between a society and an educational organisation are conceptualised using the notions of bureaucratisation and professionalisation. Finally, we have added some comments on bureaucratisation and English education, in which we have attempted to draw together some material which suggests that bureaucratisation begins in the struggles of dominant coalitions, and that these struggles might tend to hide the way in which bureaucratisation often leads more to the reproduction of an existing structure of social relations than to change.

Bureaucratisation and contemporary Britain

Throughout the book an attempt has been made to demonstrate the way in which bureaucracy and bureaucratisation are concepts which are related to the experience, practical theorising, interests and commitments of man in industrial society, and that as such they are infused with meaning and value. The sociological enterprise has then been shown to be an attempt to conceptualise the concepts of man, so that these concepts too have been caught up in the debates about sociological analysis and the value commitments which underlie them. Following the work of Alan Dawe, the appropriateness of a sociological framework which emphasizes action and process, and which assumes the problem of control behind the analysis has been indicated. Thus we are interested in the meanings which men attach to their world, and the way that they attempt to impose these meanings upon others through interaction.

It has been argued that it is appropriate in such a sociological framework to use the concept of bureaucratisation to capture the process of penetration of everyday activities by the administrative structures which are activated by dominant coalitions. Its use can also be, as it was for Max Weber, the basis of a critical analysis of a whole industrial society, and not just of complex organisations in such a society. In this last chapter the outline of a critical analysis of contemporary Britain will be attempted. This enterprise starts with the assumption that bureaucratisation is not to be seen as a process which lies completely outside man's control. For while many may see increasing bureaucratisation as an inevitable trend in the future, what we must not overlook is that such a process is not in itself the primary cause of the existing distribution of power and control in a society. If we live in a society where powerlessness and subordinacy seem to be the condition of the vast majority, this is not imposed on us entirely by bureaucratisation, but by the structure of social relations which is to be found in our society. Indeed it has already been suggested in the previous chapter that bureaucratisation starts in the conflicts between dominant coalitions, that as a process it leads to the reproduction of the class structure of social relations and, by implication, that the dominant coalitions are able to maintain their dominance. For Britain we want to show that the class structure is a product of the economic character of the society. At the same time it will be inferred that arguments to the effect that democratisation and bureaucratisation are opposing processes, and that to provide conditions for creating 'the good society' in Britain, we only have to remove the more blatant bureaucratic restrictions, are misleading. The major problem of Britain is a problem of control, but the answers to this problem tend to lie in the direction of changing the economic order and the constraints that this imposes on our society in the form of the class structure of social relations, rather than in making bureaucracy more humane or increasing the level of grass roots participation, important as these may be in themselves as intermediate goals.

The chapter consists of three main sections. The first will indicates the capitalist basis of the economic order, and the class structure which is founded in it. The second attempts to elucidate the meanings which people attach to our society, particularly with reference to work situations as a consequence of their class position, and suggests how bureaucratisation becomes involved in these meanings. Finally we return to the question of power in Britain, for as we have noted, ultimately questions about bureaucratisation are questions about power.

BRITAIN AND CAPITALISM

Britain as an industrial country for two hundred years has

undergone many changes as a consequence of urbanisation and the application of science and technology to many areas of economic and social enterprise. Fundamentally, however, the economic system still retains one characteristic which has marked it over those two centuries—it is still largely geared to the production of goods and services for private profit, and such profit tends to accrue to a very small proportion of the total population. This is not to deny that there is some state intervention in economic enterprise, indeed it is growing, and is based on notions of nationalisation, planning and funding the economy so that it will serve publicly agreed objectives. The impact of such intervention has not, however, altered the structure of social relations consequent on the inequalities in the distribution of wealth and ownership.

There are different views about this. In the 1950s one of the most influential views concerning the nature of the system was that of Anthony Crosland, who in his book *The Future of Socialism* argued that Britain had become a 'post-capitalist' society.[1] He contrasted the 1950s in Britain, which he described as a collectivist society, with what he termed the 'old' capitalism of the nineteenth century:

1. In the old, there was autonomy of economic life, complete *laissezfaire*, but now the political authority, the state, through fiscal and physical controls, ultimately held the reins.
2. Formerly, at the level of the unit of production decisions were taken by owner-managers—the capitalists—whereas now, in large jointstock enterprises, decision-making was a group procedure carried out by managers, normally divorced from contact with the owners and shareholders.
3. Then, industrial capital was privately owned, and while that was still largely true, the state controlled and taxed such capital to some extent, so that private ownership of capital had come to mean less in terms of the direction of the enterprise.
4. In the old capitalist system, the distribution of wealth was very unequal, with capitalists retaining tremendous economic power as well as using much wealth for reinvestment. Since then, the

distribution was becoming much more even, with unearned income forming a smaller proportion of the total income.

5. The ideology leading to the economic enterprise of early capitalism was based on a veneration of individualism and competition and the rights of property, and a belief in the exercise of these rights being in the best interests of the community's welfare. Such an ideology had now declined and there was more inclination to test enterprise according to whether it produced growth in wealth, and to recognise the need to sanction private enterprise.

6. A deeply held class antagonism prevailed, to the extent of virtual class war at times, in the old system, but in the collectivist state, there had been a moderation of such attitudes and there was less bitterness.

Crosland has admitted to being somewhat complacent about the changes which had taken place and the possibilities of the future,[2] and others have stressed the inadequacy of a view which seemed to overlook the characteristics of the new or advanced form of capitalism which was emerging after the second world war. In particular, two important facts can be cited to support the view that capitalism has simply taken on new forms and that the social structure of contemporary Britain has not been transformed. The first is the growing concentration of economic power in the hands of a small number of very large organisations, often multinational in their sphere of operations. The second is the continuing great disparity in the distribution of personal wealth.[3]

It can be shown that through mergers and takeovers, industrial and commercial organisations in Britain have fallen into the control of a smaller number of large companies. In 1963 it was estimated that a third of the total labour force in manufacturing industries and about 50 per cent of the capital expenditure were controlled by 180 firms. Since then, in a decade of further concentration, the basis of economic power has become even narrower. The controlling interests of such companies are also very often held by groups outside Britain, who can command the use of assets as large as those of smaller industrial states.[4] It is not unreasonable to suggest that large corporations can pursue profits and growth without concern for national interests or social responsibility if they choose to do so, that the present countervailing measures in the hands of the state are inadequate to control the power of modern capitalism, and indeed, that by and large the state is concerned more to adapt to the demands of this capitalism than to control it. It should be said also that far from there being a decline of ideology as Crosland suggested, a more pervasive ideology of increasing consumption and modernisation has emerged and is spread by the media of mass communication, often controlled by the owners of large corporations, so that new demands and rising expectations are created. This ideology tends to hide the fact the distribution of wealth, rather than becoming more even, may be becoming more polarised.

With regard to the issue of the distribution of wealth there are conflicting views, based on the difficulties of finding out how much individuals and private groups actually own, despite legislation and taxation. The profession of accountancy has to some extent grown rich on the business of helping people to interpret the legislation in their own interests. Some would go as far as to claim that they are helping to operate a tax avoidance industry.[5] Certainly Michael Meacher has calculated that annually in Britain, tax avoidance robs the state of some £800 million, and that what redistribution of wealth is taking place is mainly from rich to rich. He has also calculated that 'the richest one per cent of tax payers emerged as owning 40 per cent of total wealth, two per cent as owning 55 per cent and seven per cent as owning 84 per cent'.[6] This conflicts with the estimates of the Central Statistical Office whose calculations are hedged with many qualifications, which Meacher has attempted to account for in his estimates.[7] Nevertheless, both sets of estimates draw the same conclusions, that wealth is very unevenly distributed and that what redistribution is taking place is not proceeding very rapidly.

If we accept this analysis of the continued existence, perhaps in an advanced form, of capitalism, we can see that here are still the basic conditions for a class structured society. The growing concentration of economic power and the maintenance of a very unequal distribution of wealth provide the basis for the reproduction of small economic elite groups and large groups of labourers by hand and brain standing in an opposite position to each other with regard to the control of the economic process. This dichotomy must not be taken to imply that these two sets of people are continually in conflict with each other, or that within the set that is relatively powerless to control the economic process, all will attach the same meaning to their situation. There are certainly middle-class groups who through their skills and relative wealth can preserve an image of autonomy, which nevertheless is easily exploded by the movement of emphasis in trade and industry, as the numbers of redundant managers amongst the large numbers of unemployed in the 1970s tends to suggest. On the whole, however, as agents and privileged users of the capitalist state and its economic system, they do enjoy protection from the crises of that system. On the other hand the class of industrial workers is characterised by relatively uncertain incomes and is more exposed to the vicissitudes of economic life. It is from it by and large that the unemployed, the aged poor, the chronically destitute and the 'claimants' are drawn, and obviously they do not enjoy the same opportunities as the others in terms of education and social services. It is also from the class of industrial workers that, despite the ideology of mass consumption and rising expectations, and perhaps even because of this ideology in some cases, a labour movement continues to press an opposition to ruling economic elites through political parties and trades unions.

Thus while it may be hazardous to draw too many conclusions from the existence of a basic dichotomy in our capitalist society, we have to see that the social structure is constructed around it and the meanings or the social consciousness of its members are greatly influenced by it. In the second part of this chapter we therefore explore these meanings particularly with reference to work situations, but at the same time note how bureaucratisation is involved in them.

WORK AND THE PENETRATING INFLUENCE OF BUREAUCRATISATION
The inequality of work
The world of work in industry in Britain can provide us both with our hints of the predominant meanings and with some assessment of the part that bureaucratisation plays. On the one hand, work is the accepted basis on which man is assessed and placed in society by himself and others; it forms his major label. Not only does it mean an income, it also means an identifiable status and the possibility of being able to have self-respect. Hence the considerable agony which is felt as the threat of unemployment grows, and the concern that is shown by workers at all times to preserve work opportunities. Most collective attempts at work demarcation, work sharing and maintenance of employment by workers derive basically from the sense of work as the activity which makes them 'men', and gives them, therefore, an identity around which other expectations can be met.[8] Work provides the most continuous experience in adult life in which expectations developed in earlier life can be tested and tried, and through which individually and collectively planned projects may be realised or confounded. The experience of work is potentially the most significant area of life for confirming or refuting the possibilities which individuals and groups come to hold through earlier and continuing socialisation.

On the other hand, as we have already noted, the ultimate control of work situations tends to be increasingly concentrated in the hands of a small but powerful elite, whose private interests tend to dominate the organisation of work. To some extent public ownership, that is, the exercise of some state control over the organisation and direction of work, adds a complicating factor, making the separation of British people into 'workers' and 'owners' virtually impossible. Nevertheless, almost the same principle of profitability applies to both public and private work organisation and this entails the separation of economically active people in industrial work into governors and governed, or managers and the managed, the governors 'ideally' making the decisions as to the employment of raw materials, capital and the governed in what seem to be the most cost-effective ways. The management of the governed, particularly in view of the considerable trend for industrial concerns to be enlarged in the interests of securing and maintaining profitability and growth, has also increasingly become subject to the process of bureaucratisation. This does not follow the same pattern in every organisation, but an obvious consequence arises because the common way of ensuring or attempting to ensure the compliance of the hierarchically differentiated managers in the enterprise is the payment of incrementally increasing salaries and the granting of various privileges and benefits according to status. The result is of course the perpetuation of a considerable measure of inequality.[9]

The fact of increasing bureaucratisation is indicated roughly by the growth of non-manual occupations in the economy, the proportion increasing from 19 per cent to 36 per cent over fifty years.[10] Organisational sponsorship, both in terms of offering higher identifiable status and better expectations and conditions of work than for manual workers and other managed groups, is indicated in the continuing gap between non-manual and manual workers' earnings. The greater variation in the earnings of non-manual workers than of manual workers, is also to some extent an indication of the importance of hierarchies and career expectations among the managers, although it also indicates the existence of large distinctions in this sector, as for instance between female clerical staff and male management staff (see above, pp. 24–5).[11] Table 1 summarises some interesting indications of the variation in the organisational sponsorship of managers and the managed derived from research by Wedderburn and Craig.[12]

It seems important to note at this point that such evidence while clearly indicating some of the considerable consequences of bureaucratisation for the regulation of differential work experiences, does not contradict the point that it is only a secondary phenomenon in relation to the origins of meanings and consciousness. More fundamental seems to be the continuing reproduction of the structure of social relations in Britain, through bureaucratisation. Both in the recruitment of workers to the different levels of management and managed, and in the confirmation of life

TABLE 1 *Terms and conditions of employment — per cent of establishments in which various conditions apply*

	operatives	foremen	clerical workers	technicians	Middle managers	Senior managers
Holidays: 15 days +	38	72	74	77	84	88
Choice of holiday time	35	54	76	76	84	88
Normal working 40+ hours per week	97	94	9	23	27	22
Sick pay—employers' scheme	57	94	98	97	98	98
Pension—employers' scheme	67	94	90	94	96	96
Time off with pay for personal reasons	29	84	83	86	91	93
Pay deductions for any lateness	90	20	8	11	1	0
Warning followed by dismissal for persistent lateness	84	66	78	71	48	41
No clocking on or booking in	2	46	48	45	81	94

Source: D. Wedderburn, 'Inequality at Work' in P. Townsend and N. Bosanquet, ed., *Labour and Inequality*, Fabian Society, 1972, p. 177.

experiences and possibilities, the organisation of work reflects the constraints of the class structure. Recruitment into managerial levels, for instance, is considerably in favour of people with middle-class backgrounds (see below, especially Tables 2 and 3). Confirmation of life experiences and possibilities tends towards fulfilling for those of middle-class origins, status mobility expectations or at least some semblance of status and power maintenance, while for those of working-class origins, the confirmation is in terms of lower status, relative powerlessness, lack of control over social institutions and threatened insecurity, especially in periods of increasing unemployment and redundancy.[13]

Collective employee activities
The confirmation of class expectations is not simply a consequence of organisational sponsorship, for there are in some ways complementary and in other ways countervailing activities in collective employee associations. There are, it seems, four important points to make.

1. The view of collective employee activity as being entirely in conflict with that of management and employer is a common starting assumption both in sociology and in the mass media, but it is one which overlooks the possibility that such collective activity can operate both to confirm the class-based expectations of participants at some times and at other times to confound them. Thus participation in trade union activity may well confirm a worker in his working-class status and through contact in negotiation with employers and managers socialise him into acceptance of the class structure of social relations. At other times workers may experience, as we note below, a reversal of the 'us—them' model and find themselves in control, either in the administration of such collective activity or in the progress of some action in defiance of management.

2. Collective employee activity may not be confined to those of lowest status. So-called 'white-collar' union activity has been recognised as an important phenomenon of recent times in the formation of clerical, banking, technical, managerial and scientific

worker unions. The purpose of such unionisation may on the one hand be related to perceived threats to livelihood through mergers of organisations, career blockage, technological change and trade recessions, that is, to the emergence of a consciousness of affinity with the situation of all employee groups, on the other hand it may also be concerned with the maintenance and improvement of status and career lines and the attempt to preserve gaps between 'white' and 'blue-collar' unions. There are obviously many links between 'white-collar' union activity and professionalisation, discussed in the last chapter, and the point made there about the dialectical relationship between professionalisation and bureaucratisation would seem transferable to the situation of most employee activity in relation to work organisations.

3. Collective employee activity is a response from groups of workers attempting to realise themselves in work, and usually starts from a definition of lack of control over the work situation in consequence of decisions made by elite members of an organisation or of the environmental conditions of the organisation. It may, therefore, be brought about by bureaucratic procedures which have heightened the experience of what Marx, Weber and others have called alienation. It may equally be activated by the sheer cussedness of employers or managers refusing to accept employees as human beings. It may also be engendered by employees' definitions of what is unacceptable in terms of work possibilities, payments and conditions of work.

4. Such activity, over time, tends to become organised into relatively large unions or associations. To a considerable extent such large unions have tended to become bureaucratised, through the attempt to make links between elected and appointed leaders and the members, and to ensure the pursuit of all agreed policies. In a sense, therefore, they mirror the capitalist organisations to which they are responding, and also in the same ways may become bound by procedure, formal lines of communication, hierarchical structuring and the development of departmentalisation.[14] One of the consequences of this is the tendency of workers at the shop floor level and their elected representatives the shop stewards at

the first level of the union hierarchy, to define gaps between themselves and union officials, representing the more professionalised sections of the union structure. Evidence of this can be seen, for instance, in *The Affluent Worker* studies of Goldthorpe and Lockwood, where they noted the tendency for participation in union branch activity to be very slight compared with that in the work place.[15] Recently, too, this can be seen to have resulted in the willingness of shop stewards to form work place committees, often across the boundaries of unions involved in particular works, in order to attempt to resolve local disputes. It has become frequent enough in fact to lead some commentators to talk of a shop stewards' movement. It seems, therefore, important to examine cases of disputes where such committees have been formed, for it can be assumed that in the potential challenge which such events pose to established organisations, the roots of bureaucratisation and the varying consciousness of participants will be exposed. Two cases have been chosen which have been widely reported and studied. The first represents a situation in which the policy of a government was at least deflected if not reversed, and the second perhaps the more typical story of frustration and defeat of workers' protest.

The case of Upper Clyde Shipbuilders
Upper Clyde Shipbuilders was a company controlling five shipyards, formed with Labour Government backing in the late 1960s. Four of the five yards were threatened with closure by the Tory Government in 1971, on the basis of a prior policy of ruthless excision of so-called uprofitable industrial concerns (the 'lame duck' policy), and a report made by a committee of four men, representing industrial interests, the chairman of a Scotch whisky firm, a shipping magnate, a merchant banker and a former chairman of the National Coal Board. The workers in the threatened yards were convinced of the wrongness of this policy, not only because of the threat to their jobs but also because it was estimated that at least 30,000 other jobs in firms servicing the yards and their workers would also be in jeopardy. When the Government decided

to put an official liquidator in the company with the aim of reducing the labour force from 8,500 to 2,500, a shop stewards' committee took over the yards in what they termed a 'work-in'. On the principle of keeping open the four yards and the labour force intact, by using mass meetings and a weekly bulletin to keep all the workers involved, and by appealing to the Labour Movement nationally and internationally for funds to back them, the Committee was able to have the whole situation reviewed. After six months the Government agreed to finance three of the yards and eventually after one year an American company producing oil rigs purchased the fourth. No one who wanted to stay in the yards actually lost his job or his wage, though some left voluntarily and many were declared redundant but were able to stay because of the funds received by the shop stewards' committee.

The workers have made some concessions in gaining their end of the right to work. Apart from having to accept both a Government-backed private controlling company and another from America, thus losing what had during the work-in been effective worker control, some of the craftsmen, for example the boilermakers, have lost some of their job security in the process of making new work agreements which end some restrictive practices. It is likely that conflicts will arise again.

Nevertheless, the deflection of Government policy has meant the reduction of any legitimacy granted to their pursuance of the former course of action in the face of workers' leaders whose own legitimacy was derived perhaps from two major sources. The first was the credibility of their own analysis of the situation, which was based in the claim of the disastrous social consequences of Government policy. This credibility was achieved not only because of the contemporary fears and expectations of the workers, but also because of the experience and beliefs of an industrial community on Clydeside and beyond, which recalled earlier struggles and deprivation, when shipyards were closed in Britain, particularly in the 1930s, and saw the current rising tide of unemployment in Britain in the 1970s. The credibility was maintained despite contradictory analysis and the reiterations of the social concern of the Government and insinuations of subversion and anarchy carried by some elements of the national press or published by pressure groups like 'Aims of Industry'. But the legitimacy of the UCS shop stewards' committee was such that no attempt was made to break them either by resort to the legal process or by union hierarchies seeking to maintain their own spheres of influence.

The second source of this legitimacy was undoubtedly the manner in which the whole enterprise of the work-in was carried forward and the existence of leaders with personal qualities which enabled them to put their case with both great eloquence and persuasiveness. There was an undoubted air of authority about the way in which radio and television were used by these men and in particular the chief spokesman, Jimmy Reid. It seemed to correspond very closely to Weber's notion of charisma. As such we have no evidence of the extent to which it had any influence on the considerable determination of the Committee and the workers to secure their right to work, but it possibly did much to reinforce latent support outside Clydeside, and seems clearly to have been one component in the power struggle during the work-in. How far it would count as evidence to support either Weber or Crozier in their view of the necessity for charisma as the means of restricting the advance of bureaucratisation and 'the disenchantment of the world' is doubtful. Let us leave it in Reid's own words:

> Be that as it may, there can be little doubt that the struggle of the UCS workers, the unique form of struggle against redundancies and closures that we devised, the almost unprecedented support received from the working class movement and the wide community, is of historic importance.[16]

The strike at Pilkingtons

While the work-in is a relatively new phenomenon of industrial relations and one which is clearly very appropriate in strategies to restrict redundancies and closures, so that it is likely to become increasingly common, the more traditional form of employee final response to unwillingness of employers to concede their requests on questions of pay and conditions of work has been withdrawal of labour or the strike. Much of what follows in this second case study of the emergence of 'grass roots' resistance on the shop floor, is derived from the study by Lane and Roberts, using a social action frame of reference, of a strike lasting seven weeks in the summer of 1970 at the Pilkington Glass Company in St Helen's, Lancashire.[17]

The authors define this dispute as a 'wildcat strike'—one in which there was no official union backing and which emerged without any preceding long-term negotiations ending in stalemate. Pilkingtons and the workers' union, the General and Municipal Workers' Union (GMWU) had prided themselves before this dispute in the progressive character of industrial relations in the company, which were based on a negotiated union shop and apparently very democratic negotiating procedures. The union shop agreement meant that membership of the GMWU was a condition of employment in the company, and industrial relations were based on the workings of the Joint Industrial Council (JIC). The JIC had equality of membership of management and worker/union representatives, covered the whole of the company throughout Britain, and had a constitution which officially allowed it to discuss any matter raised by any member of the Company or Council. It became clear however that both the Union shop and the JIC had been negotiating more in terms of union and company interests than of worker and shop stewards' interests. The latter were based in the variable work situations of individual plants, where there were already complex and different scales of pay reflecting widely contrasting work conditions. The pressure for taking all disputes to a national level was a serious cause for discontent among workers and was one of the factors which the Court of Inquiry into the strike highlighted as a source of conflict.

The strike itself arose in a particularly dirty and dangerous part of one of the company works—the flat drawn department, making window glass—where a group of workers had felt for some time that they were underpaid and had tried, in their terms unsuccessfully, to bring their case to the JIC. The immediate cause of the strike was the dissatisfaction of these men when they found that they had been in their own view underpaid on Friday, 3 April 1970. The management were approached and said that this was possibly the result of a clerical error, which they were prepared to discuss immediately with a group of delegates elected by the workers, and if necessary have put right. About three hundred workers elected a number of delegates to meet the management over the issue, but at the same time decided that they should ask not just for correction of the error, but for a rise of £5 per week (what they had been claiming earlier). The management representatives, and the union official called in by the management, were amazed by this demand at the ensuing meeting that afternoon, and fell back on their constitutional position that they had no power to discuss a wage rise in the plant. The delegates reported back to workers assembled in a canteen and at this point the weeks of frustration mounted so that a motion to strike was carried easily, and arragements to press the local Union branch and other workers in St Helen's to support them were made. Despite it being a weekend, and despite the complexities of workers being involved in shift work, 8,500 men employed by Pilkingtons in St Helen's had joined the strike within forty-eight hours. By the end of the following week over 11,000 Pilkington workers in Britain were on strike, and the demand had been put up to £10 per week. There appears to have been much spontaneity and little planning in the decisions to come out. Mass meetings held in St Helen's in the first weekend were the scene of the forging of common bonds strong enough to set up powerful norms to which the majority of the workers felt they had to respond.

The local GMWU branch, one of the largest branches in Britain, and not one that had apparently been marked by a great deal of representative activity, at first seemed to show some support for the strike, but a national GMWU official, speaking at a mass meeting on its sixth day, declared that the Union would not back the strike, although it would agree to start negotiations if the men agreed to go back to work. He was shouted down, and from that moment there emerged a wave of interest in the formation of a strike committee, which could control the strike and negotiate for the men, if the Union failed to back them. In fact the GMWU through its national officers got a meeting of the JIC and accepted a £3 per week rise for all manual workers in the company, to be added to basic rates. This occurred two weeks after the strike began, without the men returning to work. This was put to workers through the branches, and though accepted elsewhere in Britain it was eventually turned down in St Helen's. By this time a Rank and File Strike Committee (RFSC) had been formed and was receiving much support in the town among the workers. Some of the members of RFSC were also official GMWU shop stewards and they went to the branch meeting when the £3 offer was discussed. Lane and Roberts report that at least two versions of what happened at the meeting were given to them. 'Loyal' GMWU stewards reported that the offer was accepted at the branch, but that it was agreed to put it to the workers at a mass meeting the next day, in the expectation that it would be accepted. RFSC stewards reported that the branch did not do any more than agree to put the offer to the men at a mass meeting without recommending acceptance or rejection. The mass meeting turned down the offer and from this time the disagreement between the RFSC and the GMWU seemed to be of more consequence than that between the workers and the company. The Union indeed was convinced that it should continue to urge the workers to settle for the £3 and return to work, while the RFSC continued to suggest that the GMWU was on the company's side and was prepared to use undemocratic means to break the strike. The RFSC held several mass meetings at which they achieved majority votes for continuing the strike, although the company refused to negotiate with them. The GMWU held ballots from which they concluded that a majority of workers wanted to go back to work in St Helen's. Both sides were therefore able with some justification to claim strong support, a fact which led to scuffles at factory gates from time to time. In the end an offer from the General Secretary of the TUC to mediate for the RFSC was accepted and the workers went back to work seven weeks after the strike had begun, accepting the £3 rise at the same time. Thereafter the company and the GMWU reasserted their dominance, resolutely refusing to discuss the situation with the RFSC because of alleged misconduct by the RFSC after the end of the dispute. The RFSC then attempted to form a breakaway union, and although officers were elected and subscriptions made, the company would not recognise them. When some of the members of the breakaway union attempted a token strike to gain recognition, the company dismissed them, offering them re-employment only if they rejoined the GMWU. Those who refused remained unemployed and their breakaway union fell apart. No other union could or would fight for them.

Lane and Roberts interpret the dispute as a product of several distinct but interacting forces, deriving from the interests of the workers, the management and the GMWU, with the Government (Labour at this time) playing a much more negative role than in the case of UCS. The Government had made some contribution in that it had abandoned its pressure on price and wage restraints some months beforehand, so that wage bargaining in the JIC was presumably easier. Department of Employment and Productivity officials were present at the meeting when the £3 offer was first agreed, signifying assent to this bargaining move, which was quite a large one at that time. Lane and Roberts also suggest that the Government had contributed much to what they term a 'strike-conscious' culture, by helping to heighten the reaction of the Press and the public to strikes as not being in the 'national interest', and this possibly did as much to foment strikes as to reduce their occurrence. Certainly the attacks which the Labour Government had made on various sections of the working classes, in attempts to maintain the 'balance of payments' or the 'credibility of the pound', did not create definitions which supported the idea that wage restraint was in the interests of a better future. Few really obvious moves had been made in the direction of greater equality.[18] During the strike, apart from sending civil servants to the JIC meeting, the Government did little except in agreeing to set up a Court of Inquiry, at the request of the RFSC, but even this did not have much effect since the dispute was 'officially' over before the court reported.

In noting the existence of worker, union and company interests, of course, it would be easy to overestimate the degree of homogeneity within these collectivities. Already, perhaps, too many liberties have been taken about the meaning of 'the Government', 'the Labour movement', 'the industrial community' and so on. To indicate the complexity of making assumptions about homogeneity, it is useful to look at the varying definitions of the situation in and about St Helen's at the time of the dispute. Lane and Roberts indicate, according to their interpretation of their observation of events and discussion with people involved in the strike, that there were at least three major worker definitions. Their description of them suggests that we might refer to them as the activist, the deferential and the quiet life definitions.

The *activist* definition maintained that the work situation needed changing because of the inequalities and the discriminations between management and employees, and between employees, and that change could only be brought about by action. Within the set of workers holding this definition were the members of the RFSC; even here there were contrasts, for they were not, as Lane and Roberts suggest, all 'hardened class warriors'. They varied according to how much change they felt was necessary and possible—some wanted complete revolution in management-worker relations, others just reform and sharing of control—and according to what kind of action should be pursued—some wanted a hard and consistently tough line, others were more conciliatory. 'Militants', 'fatalists' (activists without much faith in a better future) and 'reformers' are particularly specified by the authors. The definitions changed to some extent during the progress of the strike as most of them had not taken part in a strike before. They also changed according to the context of the discussion, so that it appears that the hard line predominated in RFSC meetings, while perhaps more conciliatory ones predominated at other times, such as the mass meetings and the Court of Inquiry proceedings. In other words there was a response to what might be termed the emergent properties of the differently structured social situations—the sets of social constraints by which people tend to be influenced according to the range of people present, their respective perceived power and status and so on.

The *deferential* definition was based in the ideas that work for the company was not at all bad, that there were pretty good relationships, and that even if there were status and pay differences, these could be explained and justified in terms of the qualities of men and the variability of work requirements. Among the set holding this definition were many of the long-service employees, some with long-standing family connections with Pilkingtons, who recognised the benefits of cooperation with management but were willing to be members of a union, and possibly be active too, because of the benefits that could also bring industry wide in terms of orderly development through encouraging the exercise of skill and discipline and providing a process for regulated relationships with managements.

The *quiet life* definition maintained that work anywhere was likely to be no more than an unfortunate necessity, but that it brought a means of enjoying a certain standard of living and that improvements in pay and conditions were worth negotiating. Holders of this definition would tend to fall into the category of the 'privatised' worker suggested by Goldthorpe and Lockwood in their studies.[19] They tended to have an instrumental attitude towards collective employee activity, supporting it if it seemed likely to bring improvements. This does not mean that they necessarily felt deep down that money and standards of living were the only reason for working, but they had come to accept this definition through experiences of socialisation which confined the view of the possibilities for them of organised work situations. They would often hold the activities of non-work situations as much more significant.

Those holding the last definition tended to be in the majority and because their definition of the work situation was mainly instrumental they formed a problem for the activists, as well as for the Union and the management, since their support for particular courses of action had to be won and could not be predicted in advance. They were the least easy to reach and communicate with during the strike, since they tended to stay at home or even find other casual work. Particularly after the £3 offer they were liable to feel that the continued strike in St Helen's was a troublesome intrusion into their normal routine. The deferentials were much more predictable and tended to be shocked by the strike, and were the least likely to give any kind of support to the RFSC. They remained 'loyal' to the GMWU.

It was among the activists that the strike was developed and maintained. For them the strike provided clear lessons in the problem of control. Lane and Roberts note:

> To some the strike was an education. . . . For these people the strike could be rightly described as a revolutionary experience. . . . To go on strike is to deny the existing distribution of power and authority. The striker ceases to respond to managerial command; he refuses to do his 'work'. A new dimension of living can thus be revealed to the striker; an existence in which 'ordinary' people are able to control events and command the attention of 'them'.[20]

It was the activists who were able to break through the crust of hardened structures and the expectations related to these, which the others accepted either willingly or under felt pressure. Having experienced liberation for a time, however, they learnt in the aftermath of the strike that 'they' had considerable powers of resilience. As one said:

> Britain is getting less and less democratic every day. We are going back to the Dark Ages, only it's being done in 1970s fashion. The days when people were persecuted, when they had their hands chopped off for petty reasons. It's now being done in a more up-to-date fashion: you get blacklisted instead so that you can't get a job anywhere. People are getting so that they want to burst out of their skins and take a swipe at somebody for having pressure put on them.[21]

Such a comment reflects both the perception of the immediate situation becoming much more limiting and hard for the RFSC member, and the way in which an experience such as this illuminates and feeds a wider consciousness of inequality—practice linking with theory to provide further confirmation of a significant definition of the situation. It also confirms the view that strikes are not just cases of deviance from a normal consensus situation, nor are motivated by solely materialistic considerations, but are something of a 'protest movement' which is concerned with the problem of control in a society where increasingly it may appear that the more we claim the fundamental democratic nature, the more it is revealed that control is vested in relatively small and highly selected dominant coalitions in government and business.

The members of the management set at Pilkingtons are more closely related to such dominant coalitions and carry the legitimating force of this connection, so that apart perhaps from slightly restructuring the approach to industrial relations after the strike they have been able to reassert their dominance and form of order almost as though nothing had happened. As Lane and Roberts point out, too, after two weeks of the strike, the management was able to 'play it cool', since the dispute tended to turn on a struggle between the GMWU and the RFSC. Nevertheless there were contrasting definitions among the managers, stemming basically from the older Pilkington style, paternalistic and familistic, depending on claimed close relations between the Pilkington family (still very much involved in the company) and the workers, and from a newer international company style, seeking legitimacy in modern methods and training, more 'objectives' oriented techniques pursued through specialised and formalised functions and supporting the idea of professionalised representation of workers through the union shop agreement with the GWMU. The older style management probably felt hurt by the strike, while the newer style managers were more realistic and ready to make adjustments, and to sponsor the Union's efforts to get the men back; this they did by helping the Union to hold the ballots and by resisting the attempt to form the breakaway union. The older style relied more on local knowledge, attempting to bring the workers back by tactics such as claiming more had returned to work than actually had, during the strike period, and possibly arranging privately with the local chief constable for a tougher police approach to the pickets. It was possibly the more bureaucratised new management style which was one of the causes of the strike, in that much more reliance was placed on reported and processed evidence. Lines of communication grew longer and there were more people and departments involved, each possibly interpreting the situation in the light of their own particular interests, so that there was no real awareness of and reaction to discontent in St Helen's and elsewhere.

There is certainly a parallel here with the way in which the GMWU operated and was caught unawares by the dispute. The parallel even extends to possibly similar conflicts between family and professional union interests. Both Lane and Roberts, and other commentators, have noted the tendency for the top positions in the GMWU to be kept in 'the family', that is for continuity to be maintained by the appointment of members who have family connections with former officials of the Union.[22] Lord Cooper, the general secretary from 1960 to 1972, is the nephew of a former general secretary, and two of his brothers are regional officials. Contenders for election to his position include one who is also a son and grandson of former officials as well as being a son-in-law of a previous general secretary, Lord Williamson. (He was in fact the elected successor, and is now general secretary.) Other potential candidates seem also to have family links with former officials and one already has a son acting as a full-time branch official. The familistic image of the Union seems also to link with a firm resolve to keep the Union moderate as far as the political spectrum is concerned, to see industrial relations much more in terms of cooperation than conflict, and to define the members more as clients than as participants. On the whole, the GMWU was thus not ready to accept the idea of members taking matters into their own hands at Pilkingtons, and certainly there was a tendency to take exception to the idea of the RFSC from the moment of its inception. As the strike progressed GMWU officials possibly made accusations of subversion and anarchy with reference to the RFSC as severe as those that appeared in the

Press. But to some extent it can be said that the union was only reflecting the way that the deferential workers saw the strike. On the other hand, one of the major problems was the tendency for full-time officers to press hard for the development of profession-alised services to members. Based in the thinking which also had initially carried along the Labour Government in the 1960s that most of Britain's social problems could be solved by modernisation and growth through the use of new technology introduced and managed by experts, the GMWU had pursued a policy of using the wealth derived from a large membership to import numerous professionals into the various departments of the Union. Expert advice perhaps in this case rebounded on them, but it seems a fair statement to suggest that the union had become the organisation and not the members, so that union officials were remote from shop floor workers.

Despite attempts to recapture the image of a democratic union, it seems probable that the GMWU is still very much organisation conscious and is interpreting the notion of democracy not through the definitions of shop floor members, but through those of the experts in the hierarchy. Thus the skills and ideas of rank and file members become data to be manipulated and used by the officials, rather than the basis of control and strategy on the shop floor. A recent advertisement, 'Unity is strength' appearing in the *Labour Weekly*[23] no doubt intended to give a trendy image, succeeds more in suggesting that what the GMWU has chiefly earned from the Pilkington strike is that where new skills become apparent among the members, such as the ability to form a Rank and File committee, then such skills are ripe for incorporation into the organisation by departmentalising and formalising them. The parallel with school counselling at Lakeshore High School (see above, pp. 92f) seems fairly clear:

UNITY IS STRENGTH

A new department of the GMWU, set up in 1970, can now see notable signs of success.

There has, in recent months, been a large increase in membership in relatively unorganised industries such as catering, and among the white collar section. This is in large part due to the work of the Union's national organisation department.

The GMWU, recognising the importance of strong shop floor union organisation for the effective representation of the membership, set up the department to develop overall recruitment strategies.

As part of this policy the department analyses employment trends and new industrial developments and supplies the appropriate regions of the Union with this information. Members of the department then assist regional officials in the field in specific recruitment campaigns analysing the local employment situation and any changes in those industries in which we are involved.

This is the type of recruitment work which 'Organisation' finds most challenging for no two situations are the same and the potential member has to be immediately convinced of the Union's ability to look after the member's interest at work.

The department also provides an ideal training ground for potential full-time regional officials. They move from the department to the regions and a continuing stream of new recruitment ideas comes from new people in the department drawn from the active rank and file of the Union.

'Organisation' is part of the Union's servicing policy for members. By successfully developing new recruitment strategies it gives practical effect to the Union's motto, 'Unity is Strength'.

What is not clear, of course, is how far effectiveness in recruiting more members means effectiveness in representation of the membership. If the tendency is to place great emphasis on the organisation as such it is very possible that the interests generated in the organisation will come to stand between the members and the solution of their problems, and indeed come to define the members' problems for them.

This study thus seems to illustrate clearly the very complex forces which can be involved in work situations. Bureaucratisation here penetrated the situation from at least two major sources and was clearly very influential in the meanings which some members of management and the union attached to the dispute. But as the study suggests these stood against the meanings which the activists attached to the conflict. Their consciousness of inequality and powerlessness also contrasted with that of other workers who seem to have been socialised in various ways to accept the possibilities that the capitalist organisation of work seemed to offer. The fundamental dichotomy, which was indicated, in the previous section, to have arisen in the class structure of our society and was shown more clearly in the case of UCS, was here made much less transparent, both through bureaucratisation and forms of socialisation common in our society. Bureaucratisation, along with other social processes, thus tends to serve to maintain the dominance of those who control the economic system, by conceding to some subordinates sponsored careers and benefits as a sanction for compliance in their agency. Even where it arises within the labour movement, it can produce the same effects, for such is the pull of individual and particular interests, that social interests can be obfuscated. It is of course part of the ideology of modern capitalism that rising expectations should be experienced through individual striving and that each and every avenue of apparent mobility should be exploited to reach out for more of the supposed benefits of the mass consumer society. In this way the power and most of the wealth remain in the hold of small groups, and failure to succeed can be individualised.

Both the above case studies also illustrate how adept dominant groups are in reasserting their overall control after periods of protest. After the UCS work-in all the workers gained was the preservation of their right to work and the removal for the time being of the threat of severe material deprivation. After the strike at Pilkingtons even the right to work was not maintained for all the workers. The latter conflict illustrated too how even a very large union may come to depend to a considerable extent on the sponsorship of a company for the power it can wield. It is therefore not surprising that collective employee activity tends to be caught up in what can be seen as the reproduction of the class structure of social relations in Britain.

If, therefore, as sociologists we are to take the side of the underdog in our value commitment, and we wish to understand the basis of social inequality and injustice in particular societies, then it would seem that in the case of Britain it is not simply bureaucratisation on which we should focus, but the class structure and the power that maintains it. Thus we turn finally to the question of power in Britain.

THE QUESTION OF POWER

It will be useful to look once more at the concept of class structure, before dealing with the question of power. The concept has here been taken to refer to the way in which people in an industrial society are differentiated economically into controllers of the means of production, that is the large-scale owners of property and wealth, and subordinates, that is workers by hand and brain, small scale businessmen, wage and salary earners, who depend on the decisions and initiatives of the controllers for their livelihood. The concept of class is intended to indicate the potentiality that controllers and subordinates will form for themselves consciously active groups seeking to achieve or maintain a differential power position in relation to control over economic and political institutions in a society. Classes are thus social formations differentiated by access to power and wealth in a society, which potentially can give rise to movements which can challenge or change the dominant order of a society. A dominant or ruling class is one which has achieved control and seeks to maintain it, through its elite members.

From this point of view the question of power resolves itself into the question of whether there is a ruling class in Britain. The argument about the answer to this question has been prolonged, because the evidence which would lead with certainty to the affirmation of a relatively uniformly recruited and established group holding centralised control, is perhaps the most difficult to obtain of all sociological enterprises. Anthony Giddens, who has outlined a research strategy for such an enterprise, ended a recent paper with the remark that:

> Concealment, subterfuge, but above all probably the ubiquity of informal and personalised relationships and procedures—something which, although no doubt common in the connections between elite groups, is likely to be much more prevalent inside them—create large blank spots which no form of sociological research is likely to penetrate.[24]

In addition there have been two significant counterhypotheses to the effect that there is no ruling class now. One states the view that the ruling class has decomposed as power has been widely diffused. Ralf Dahrendorf can be said to be an exponent of such a thesis, for he suggests that in an industrial society such as Britain, power is spread among a plurality of elites, who because of their differing functions and partially distinct reference groups potentially hold incompatible expectations of each other. Thus conflict is an essential element of the structure of society at all levels.[25] The other counterhypothesis suggests that the ruling class has been replaced by a new elite of leading professionals and managers, so that for instance there has been a complete divorce between ownership and control of trade and industry. We have already noted this in the work of Anthony Crosland (see above, p. 114) but it derives from James Burnham.[26] Both these hypotheses have had considerable support, though the evidence for them is not particularly strong. With regard to the latter, it may be said that if there is a division between ownership and control, it does not seem to be as great or as influential as that between managers and the managed. Modern managers may be more vigorous in support of the interests of the owners than the owners themselves, and their community of interest in this direction is made more pronounced by the fact that many managers are also stockholders in their own companies. It is also the policy of many large companies to invest their funds in other companies, so that ownership and management become doubly interlocked.

It is the first counterhypothesis, the decomposition thesis, which is perhaps the more persuasive, since it is possible to indicate the existence of numerous elite groups, connected with various national institutions, such as the monarchy, the peerage, parliament, large economic organisations, the judiciary, the civil service, the military, the trade unions, higher education, the mass media and the churches, and point effectively to the apparent power that each possesses, and the conflicts that occur between them.[27] Indeed it may seem that we used this very idea in the discussion about English education in chapter 5. But the important point to remember is that one significant consequence of the conflicts there was bureaucratisation and the tendency towards the reproduction of the class structure, which contradicted the notion of pluralism and equality of opportunity through education. Also, as we concluded that analysis, it might be that in the reproduction of the class structure we create the conditions in which the young sense their alienation and emerge with a consciousness that will find its expression in a lasting counterculture. How meaningful is the notion of pluralism and conflict between national elite groups, when as we have already indicated the conditions exist for the maintenance of power by a ruling class in the growing concentration of economic power, in the continuing inequality of the distribution of wealth and in the reproduction of the subordinacy of the mass of the population? Also when we look at the potential area of recruitment into such a ruling class, in the dominant coalitions of British society, there is undoubtedly a bourgeois homogeneity about it. In Tables 2 and 3, using

TABLE 2 *Indications of bourgeois homogeneity among members of dominant coalitions in Britain by father's occupation*

Father's occupation (R.G. social class)[2]	Administrative class, civil service 1967	University teachers in art and social sciences 1966	Scientific officer class, civil service 1967	Top managers 1954/5	Directors 1965	British population in social classes I and II		All economically active England and Wales 1966
						Born 1910-19	Born 1920-9	
I and II	67	60	54	72	50	67	67	18
III	23	31	39	25	40	29	28	49
IV and V	6	6	7	3	10	4	6	30
Others	3	3	3	–	–	–	–	3

Sources: 1. This table is an extract of information from the Committee under the Chairmanship of Lord Fulton, *The Civil Service* Volume 3(1), 'Social Survey of the Civil Service', a memorandum submitted by A.H. Halsey and I.M. Crewe, H.M.S.O., London, 1969. Tables 3.20 and 3.22. The last column is compiled from *the Census of England and Wales*, 1966.
2. The Registrar General's Social Classes: I Higher professional and managerial; II Intermediate professional and Management; III Lower non-manual and skilled manual; IV semiskilled manual; V unskilled manual.

TABLE 3 *Indications of bourgeois homogeneity among members of dominant coalitions in Britain by type of full-time school last attended*

Type of school	Administrative class 1967	University teachers in arts and social sciences 1966	Scientific officer class, civil service 1967	Graduate administrators in LEAs 1967	Managers of a large industrial organisation 1967	Percentages MPs 1959 Con.	Percentages MPs 1959 Lab.
LEA Modern Technical and Comprehensive Secondary	2		6	72	–	2	33
LEA Grammar	40	51	57		47	25	45
Direct grant	19	10	15	28	14		
Independent	37	22	21		36	73	22
Others	2	17	2	–	4	–	–

Sources: 1. Drawn from Fulton Committee, *op.cit.,* Tables 3.33 and 3.35, and J. Blondel, *Voters, Parties and Leaders,* Penguin Books, 1966, Fig. 8, p. 137.

indicators of social class and educational background, it is possible to infer that the dominant coalitions are not representative of the whole population in either sense. When we look too at the other elite groups not mentioned in Tables 2 and 3, using information drawn from the Public Schools Commission reports, the indications remain very similar.[28] While the proportion of fourteen-year-olds in England and Wales attending independent and direct grant grammar schools was a rather unrepresentative seven per cent of the total of such pupils attending full-time educational establishments in 1967, a proportion which has varied little over the past half century, the proportion of military leaders in the British services who had attended such schools was 70 per cent, the proportion of Church of England bishops was 81 per cent and the proportion of judges and Q.C.s was 88 per cent. There is therefore more than a hint of a uniformity which suggests the persistence of interrelationships—indeed strong evidence that 'the upper class in Britain has been able to resist with considerable success the attacks upon its economic interests, and that in this sense of having power to defend its interests it has maintained itself during the present century as a ruling class'.[29]

There is no doubt that the challenge to such a ruling class also has a firm basis in the development of the consciousness of alienation both among students in the centres of higher education and among workers such as those of UCS. To them the fundamental dichotomy is clear and the veil of opaqueness which bureaucratisation tends to throw over its existence is apparent. We must expect in the continuing problem of control, however, that the diffusion of the new social consciousness will be slow, for the pervasiveness of other forms of consciousness, based in the class structure of our capitalist society, is substantial. At least there seems no doubt that bureaucratisation is not primarily responsible for social inequality and injustice, but that the roots of such conditions lie as indicated in the economic system and the class structure of social relations which it supports. Bureaucratisation may be involved deeply in the strategy of reproducing such a class structure, but potentially it can provide the conditions in which a critical awareness of the realities of British society may lead to their replacement.

CONCLUSION

When a sociologist discusses social processes, he must take account of the point that sociology is itself involved in social processes. Bureaucracy and bureaucratisation are examples of concepts whose meaning is infused with value through the sociologist's and social thinker's own involvement in social processes. The 'images of bureaucracy' vary consequent on experience and reflection in theory. The discussion of Max Weber's work and of the debates with Weber, which have contributed to the construction of sociological analysis about bureaucracy, attempted to outline the main currents of value which penetrate this analysis. Using the seminal work of Alan Dawe, these were suggested to be the product of the tensions created by two chief problems—those of order and control—at the substantive and analytical levels of sociological work.

Contemporary sociology, it is claimed, should now primarily be concerned with the problem of control—how do individuals and groups control the social institutions of which they are part?—and therefore begin to articulate an action frame of reference in which the concepts of meaning and control claim analytical priority. Within this frame, the actors and their definitions of the situation—emerging through socialisation from the tensions of interests and goals with the constraints and pressures of social structure and culture—take a central place. Bureaucratisation in such a framework is not just an inevitability but an active process in which actors in dominant coalitions impose their meanings onto everyday life, through structures of administrative control, so that they separate out, sanction and define the subordinacy of men as functionaries in their world. The consequences of this, along with some description of the process itself, have been surveyed with reference to the English education system and contemporary British society. In particular it has been suggested that such a process contributes chiefly to the reproduction of the class structure of social relations in Britain, which itself is based in a capitalist economy. The emergence of the state as an important influence in the capitalist economy and the use of scientific and technological skills through professionalised occupational groups, has not seriously challenged or altered the control structure. This still lies in the hands of what is claimed to be a ruling class, recruited from dominant coalitions possessing a marked bourgeois homogeneity and formed in the interests of capitalism, rather than a set of elite groups amongst whom competition and bargaining have reached a point where the dispersion of power can be said to be on the horizon.

The emergence of new meanings or a new social consciousness always seems possible in the light of continued movements derived from the experience of alienated individuals and groups— workers, students and even career blocked professionals. But it is perhaps in the tendency for movements to become ossified and in the apparently infinitely large number of responses made by, and possibilities open to, the ruling class that such movements seem to be deflected from their intention to transform British society in fundamental ways. The social process of bureaucratisation should not, however, be seen only as a force preventing transformation. It is in the tensions produced by this and other related processes such as urbanisation, advanced industrialisation and professionalisation, channelling and perhaps constraining the attempts of individuals and groups to achieve desired goals, that we must also see the production and reproduction of social consciousness. Sociological analysis must continue to penetrate and explain such forces, make clear the basis of tensions and open up lines of action in the interest of the emergence of new meanings and new forms of control.

References and further reading

CHAPTER I. INTRODUCTION
1. Albrow, M., *Bureaucracy*, Macmillan, 1970, p. 125.
2. M.A. Coulson, and D.S. Riddell, *Approaching Sociology: a critical introduction*, Routledge, 1970, p. 7.
3. A. Dawe, 'The two sociologies', *British Journal of Sociology* vol. 21, no. 2, June 1970.
4. See Albrow, pp. 84–105.
5. R. Michels, *Political Parties*, New York, Collier Books, 1962.
6. The most recent English translation of much of Weber's work on Bureaucracy is contained in Max Weber, *Economy and Society; an outline of interpretive Sociology*, ed. G. Roth and C. Wittich, New York, Bedminster Press, 3 vols, 1968 (based on the 4th German edition). See Albrow, pp. 37–49 for his discussion about Weber's concepts.
7. P.M. Blau and M.W. Meyer, *Bureaucracy in Modern Society*, 2nd edn, Random House, 1971, p. 4.
8. *Ibid.*, pp. 167–8.
9. Coulson and Riddell, p. 9, *q.v.* for a fuller discussion of the relevance of values in sociology.
10. *Ibid.*, p. 71.

CHAPTER 2. IMAGES OF BUREAUCRACY
1. Department of Education and Science, Committee on Higher Education, *Report on Higher Education*, Cmnd 2154, HMSO, 1963 (the Robbins Report).
2. The negotiations which led to this situation were embodied at an official level in the work of a study group set up by the

Department of Education and Science to look at the government of colleges of education. The study group contained representatives of local authorities, college and university teachers, as well as of the Department of Education and Science. It was chaired by T. Weaver, of DES, and its *Report on the Government of Colleges of Education* was published by HMSO in 1966. This is a crucial document for anyone concerned with the development of the so-called binary policy of higher education in Britain.

3. This concept is derived from J. Child, 'Organizational structure, environment and performance', *Sociology*, vol. 6, no. 1 Jan. 1972. 'It refers to those who collectively happen to hold most power over a particular period of time . . . and need not imply that other members of an organization do not have some power.'

4. Association of Teachers in Colleges and Departments of Education (ATCDE), *Statement of Executive Committee on Student Participation in College Government*, published in 1968.

5. This editorial appeared at the beginning of the same academic year as the ATCDE executive statement was published. The issue was marked no. 18, September 1967. The editor was a student. Names and source are withheld to preserve the anonymity of the College.

6. Several full analyses of the theory and practice involved in student activism and staff and student relations in establishments of higher education have been written. Students might try:

    A. Cockburn and R. Blackburn, *Student Power*, Penguin Books, 1969.

    Students and Staff of Hornsey College of Art, *The Hornsey Affair*, Penguin Books, 1969.

    The Select Committee on Education and Science, *Student Relations*, vol. 1, HMSO, 1969 (H.C. 449–i).

7. J. Grimond, M.P., 'What it's all about?', *Guardian*, 21 May 1968.

8. T.N., 'Notes towards the definition of anti-culture', in *The Hornsey Affair* p. 24.

9. See M. Holland, 'Student power', *The Observer* 21 Jan. 1968.

10. A. Coote, 'The shallow end', *The Observer Review*, 25 Jan. 1972.

11. H.S. Becker, *Sociological Work, Method and Substance*, Allen Lane, The Penguin Press, 1971, pp. 123–34.

12. A. Solzhenitsyn, *Cancer Ward*, trans. N. Bethell and D. Burg, Penguin Books, 1971, pp. 208–9.

13. F. Kafka, *The Castle*, trans. W. Muir and E. Muir Penguin Books, 1971, pp. 59–60.

14. Z. Bauman, 'Uses of information: When social information becomes desired', *The Annals of the American Academy of Political and Social Science*, vol. 393, Jan. 1971, pp. 26–7.

15. Quoted in S. Avineri, *The Social and Political Thought of Karl Marx*, Cambridge University Press, 1968, pp. 23–4.

16. *Ibid*. pp. 49–51.

17. G. Lichtheim, *Marxism in Modern France*, Columbia University Press, 1966, p. 187.

18. M. Djilas, *The New Class*, Thames & Hudson, 1957. See Albrow *Bureaucracy*, 67–79, for a fuller discussion.

CHAPTER 3. SOCIOLOGISTS AND BUREAUCRACY

1. Dawe, 'The two sociologies', pp. 207–18.

2. See Coulson and Riddell, *Approaching Sociology*, p. 51.

3. Dawe, p. 212.

4. *Ibid*.

5. See for instance, K. Hope, 'Path analysis: supplementary procedures', *Sociology*, vol. 5, no. 2, May 1971, pp. 225–41, and L. Taylor, 'The significance and interpretation of replies to motivational questions: the case of sex offenders', *Sociology* vol. 6, no. 1, Jan. 1972, pp. 23–40.

   For a criticism of mathematical paradigms and for a discussion of the problems of elucidating meanings, see A. Cicourel, *Method and Measurement in Sociology*, New York, Free Press, 1964.

6. A. Dawe, 'The relevance of values', in A. Sahay, ed., *Max Weber and Modern Sociology*, Routledge, 1971, pp. 37–66.

7. D. Wrong, ed., *Max Weber*, Prentice-Hall, 1970, p. 16.

8. Dawe, 'The relevance of values', p. 50.

9. Quoted in J.P. Mayer, *Max Weber and German Politics*, Faber, 1956, pp. 127–8.

10. A.W. Gouldner, 'Anti-Minotaur: the myth of a value-free sociology', *Social Problems*, vol. 9, 1962, pp. 199–213.

11. See Chapter 1, note 6.

12. Gouldner, A.W., *op. cit.* 1962, page 204.

CHAPTER 4. AFTER WEBER

1. J. Rex, 'Typology and objectivity: a comment on Weber's four sociological methods', in Sahay; *Max Weber and Modern Sociology*, p. 34.

2. Dawe, 'The relevance of values', p. 63.

3. Albrow, *Bureaucracy*, pp. 61–2.

4. R.K. Merton, 'Bureaucratic structure and personality', in his *Reader in Bureaucracy*, New York, Free Press, 1952.

5. The references here were to F.J. Roethlisberger and W.J. Dickson, *Management and the Worker*, Harvard University Press, 1941, and C.I. Barnard, *The Functions of the Executive*, Harvard University Press, 1940.

6. P. Selznick, 'An approach to a theory of bureaucracy', *American Sociological Review*, vol. 8, no. 1, 1943, pp. 47–54.

7. T. Parsons, *The Social System*, New York, Free Press, 1951.

8. R. Bendix, *Higher Civil Servants in American Society*, University of Colorado Studies, 1949.

9. Blau and Meyer, *Bureaucracy in Modern Society*, pp. 25–6.

10. Albrow, pp. 64–5.

11. Parsons, see the criticism of this work in J. Rex, *Key Problems of Sociological Theory*, Routledge, 1961, pp. 103–12.

12. R. Aron, *Eighteen Lectures on Industrial Society*, Weidenfeld & Nicolson, 1967, pp. 22 and 28.

13. See, for instance, A. Etzioni, *Complex Organizations; a sociological reader*, Holt, Rinehart & Winston, New York, 1964; D.S. Pugh, *Organization Theory, Selected Readings*, Penguin Books, 1971; and D.S. Pugh *et al.*, *Writers on Organizations*, Penguin Books, 1971.

14. See C.R. Hinings *et al.*, 'An approach to the study of bureaucracy', *Sociology*, vol. 1, no. 1, Jan. 1967, 61–72.

15. S.A. Stouffer, L. Guttman, P. Lazarsfeld *et al.*, *Studies in Social Psychology in World War II*, vol. 4 *Measurement and Prediction*, Princeton University Press, 1950.

16. Hinings, p. 61.

17. See Dawe, p. 52.

18. A useful summary of the ethnomethodological position can be found in H.P. Dreitzel, *Recent Sociology no. 2, Patterns of Communicative Behaviour*, New York, Macmillan, 1970.

19. Cicourel, *Method and Measurement in Sociology*, p. 36. This passage also indicates that ethnomethodologists can make starting assumptions, too, which suggest at least some reification of concepts.

20. Another implication is, of course, that the sociological enterprise is bureaucratised; on this, see C.W. Mills, *The Sociological Imagination*, Penguin Books, 1970, especially ch. 5.

21. Cicourel, p. 133.

22. M. Crozier, *The Bureaucratic Phenomenon*, Tavistock, 1964.

23. A. Cicourel and J.I. Kitsuse, *The Educational Decision Makers*, Bobbs-Merrill, 1963.

24. Hinings *et al.*, p. 64.

25. *Ibid.* p. 65.

26. C.R. Hinings and G.L. Lee, 'Dimensions of organisation structure and their context: a replication', *Sociology*, vol. 5, no. 1, Jan. 1971, p. 84.

27. See Hinings *et al.* for a discussion about the indicators used for 'specialisation'.

28. Hinings and Lee, p. 90.

29. D.S. Pugh, D.J. Hickson, and C.R. Hinings, 'An empirical taxonomy of structures of work organizations', *Administrative Science Quarterly*, vol. 14, p. 115–26.
30. Child, *op. cit.*, (see note 3, Chapter 2.)
31. T. Burns and G.M. Stalker, *The Management of Innovation*, Tavistock, 1961.
32. He refers briefly to informal interviews with workers in the Tobacco Monopoly, and to more intensive focused interviews with the managerial teams; Crozier, *The Bureaucratic Phenomenon*, pp. 59–60.
33. Crozier, p. 158.
34. *Ibid.*, p. 187.
35. *Ibid.*, p. 194.
36. *Ibid.*, pp. 303–4.
37. *Ibid.*, p. 176.
38. A.W. Gouldner, *Patterns of Industrial Bureaucracy*, Routledge, 1955, p. 16.
39. See A.W. Gouldner, *The Coming Crisis of Western Sociology*, Heinemann, 1971, on his ideas of a reflexive sociology.

CHAPTER 5. BUREAUCRATISATION AND EDUCATION

1. Weber, *Economy and Society*, i, pp. 54–5.
2. R. Miliband, *The State in Capitalist Society*, Weidenfeld & Nicolson, 1968, pp. 49–55.
3. E. Durkheim, *Education and Sociology*, New York, The Free Press, 1956, p. 71.
4. *Ibid.*, p. 81.
5. Weber, iii, 999.
6. *Ibid.*, iii, 1000.
7. *Ibid.*, iii, 1002.
8. An attempt to explain educational change in this way drawing upon the Weberian analysis has recently been published. See M. Vaughan and M. Scotford-Archer, *Social Conflict and Educational Change, in England and France, 1789–1848*, Cambridge University Press, 1971.

9. I. Meszaros, *Marx's Theory of Alienation*, London, Merlin, 1970; see especially chapter 10, 'Alienation and the crisis of education'.

10. *Ibid.*, pp. 289, 299.

11. *Ibid.* p. 290.

12. See T. Parsons, 'The school class as a social system', in A.H. Halsey, J. Floud and C.A. Anderson, eds, *Education, Economy and Society*, New York, Free Press, 1961, pp. 434–55.

13. F. Musgrove and P.H. Taylor, *Society and the Teacher's Role*, Routledge 1969, pp. 1–2.

14. F. Musgrove, *Patterns of Power and Authority in English Education*, Methuen, 1971, p. 13.

15. See R.G. Corwin, *A Sociology of Education*, Appleton-Century Crofts, 1965; C.E. Bidwell, '*The School as a Formal Organization*', in J.G. March, *Handbook of Organizations* Rand, McNally, 1965; O. Banks, *The Sociology of Education*, Batsford, 1968; and D. Swift, *The Sociology of Education*, Routledge, 1969.

16. A. Etzioni, *A Comparative Analysis of Complex Organizations*, New York, Free Press, 1961, p. 12.

17. Several examples of this kind are contained in the set of readings in M. Craft, ed., *Family, Class and Education*, Longman, 1970.

18. Material on this point can be found in B.J. Biddle and E.J. Thomas, *Role Theory, Concepts and Research*, Wiley, 1966, especially Part 8, pp. 273–310.

19. See N. Gross, W.S. Mason and A.W. McEachern, *Explorations in Role Analysis*, Wiley, 1958.

20. The term 'college' is here used in the American sense of an institution of full-time education leading to first degrees, taking students at the age of eighteen.

21. Cicourel and Kitsuse, *The Educational Decision Makers*.

22. Extract from a comment of General William Westmoreland, to a Congressional committee, in Washington, quoted in the *New Statesman*, 30 June 1972, p. 889.

23. See H.M. Vollmer and D.L. Mills, *Professionalization*, Prentice-Hall, 1966, especially pp. 264–94.
24. In 1971 there were three ministers, twenty senior civil servants (Under Secretary and above) and about five hundred inspectors; the total staff of DES was over 4000.
25. B. Simon, *Education and the Labour Movement 1870–1920*, Lawrence & Wishart, 1965, p. 363.
26. Royal Commission on Local Government in England, *Minutes of Evidence 5*, HMSO, 1969, p. 95, para. 457.
27. National Association of Divisional Executives for Education, *Review* May 1972, p. 54.
28. See E. Boyle, A. Crosland and M. Kogan, *The Politics of Education*, Penguin Books, 1971.
29. Select Committee of the House of Commons on Education and Science, Session 1969/70, *Minutes of Evidence*, vol. I, HMSO, 1970, para. 1427.
30. The elaboration of these meanings links back to some of the points raised in the earlier part of this chapter, in the discussion of Durkheim, Weber and Meszaros, and the extracts from the work of Musgrove.
31. See Simon, *Education and the Labour Movement*, and E. Halévy, *Imperialism and the Rise of Labour*, Benn, 1961, especially pp. 139–210.
32. Evidence of this phenomenon is contained in Halsey *et al.*, *Education, Economy and Society*, 1961, Banks, *The Sociology of Education*, and B. Jackson and D. Marsden, *Education and the Working Class*, Penguin Books, 1966.
33. See on this J.C.B. Lunn, *Streaming in the Primary School*, London, NFER, 1970.
34. See, for instance, D. Marsden, 'Politicians, equality and comprehensives', in P. Townsend and N. Bosanquet, eds., *Labour and Inequality*, Fabian Society, 1972, pp. 108–42.
35. Boyle, Crosland and Kogan, p. 188.
36. *Ibid.*, p. 177.
37. Public Schools Commission, *First Report*, vols I and II, HMSO, 1968.

CHAPTER 6. BUREAUCRATISATION AND CONTEMPORARY BRITAIN

1. A. Crosland, *The Future of Socialism*, Methuen, 1956, pp. 62–7.
2. A. Crosland, *A Social Democratic Britain*, Fabian Society, 1971.
3. See for instance the analyses of R. Williams, ed., *May Day Manifesto 1968*, Penguin Books, 1968; Miliband, *The State in Capitation Society*, and J.H. Westergaard, 'Sociology: the myth of classlessness', in R. Blackburn, ed., *Ideology in Social Science*, Collins, Fontana, 1972.
4. See C. Tugendhat, *The Multinationals*, Eyre & Spottiswoode, 1971.
5. This point was made by Michael Meacher, MP, in an article in the *New Statesman*, 16 April 1971, entitled 'Mr Barber's wink to the rich'.
6. M. Meacher, 'Wealth: Labour's Achilles heel', in Townsend and Bosanquet, pp. 192–3.
7. See Central Statistical Office, *Social Trends*, HMSO, 1972.
8. See R. Fraser, *Work*, vol. 2, Penguin Books, 1969, 'Introduction' pp. 7–20.
9. See D. Wedderburn, 'Inequality at work', in Townsend and Bosanquet, pp. 174–85.
10. *Ibid.*, p. 174. See also J. Raynor, *The Middle Class*, Longman, 1969, for a summary of the growth of middle-class occupations and the implications of this growth.
11. The Department of Employment and Productivity, *Gazette*, monthly, gives the current rates of pay of British workers.
12. Wedderburn, p. 177.
13. A useful discussion of working-class life and expectations is to be found in G. Rose, *The Working Class*, Longman, 1968.
14. See for instance, V.L. Allen, *The Sociology of Industrial Relations*, Longman, 1971, pp. 54–5.
15. J.H. Goldthorpe *et al.*, *The Affluent Worker*, vol. 1, '*Industrial Attitudes and Behaviour*', Cambridge University Press, 1968.
16. In W. Thompson and F. Hart, *The UCS Work-In*, Lawrence & Wishart, 1972, p. 7. Other information was from this book.

17. T. Lane and K. Roberts, *Strike at Pilkingtons*, Collins, Fontana, 1971.
18. This is the combined judgment of the authors of the Fabian Essays contained in Townsend and Bosanquet.
19. See, for instance, D. Lockwood, 'Sources of variation in working class images of society', *The Sociological Review*, vol. 14, no. 3, Nov. 1966. In this article, Lockwood suggests a threefold division somewhat similar to that which emerges from Lane and Roberts' case study.
20. Lane and Roberts, pp. 104–5.
21. *Ibid.*, p. 202.
22. See for instance, P. Paterson, 'All in the family', *New Statesman*, 26 July 1972, p. 116.
23. *Labour Weekly*, 1 Sept. 1972, p. 6.
24. A. Giddens, 'Elites in the British class structure', *The Sociological Review*, vol. 20., no. 2, Summer 1972.
25. R. Dahrendorf, *Class and Class Conflict in Industrial Society*, Routledge, 1959.
26. J. Burnham, *The Managerial Revolution*, Putnam, 1943.
27. Giddens.
28. Public Schools Commission, *First Report* i, 59.
29. T. Bottomore, *Elites and Society*, Penguin Books, 1964, p. 40.

Index